Karen Ehman's blog was one of the first I ever read, and she's never stopped being a mentor to me. Her words here speak my heart language—and echo the heart of God. Live these words. Repeat. Have a profoundly beautiful life right where you are.

—Ann Voskamp, *New York Times*
bestselling author of *One Thousand
Gifts* and *The Broken Way*

With all the criticism and combativeness we witness online and in person, *Listen, Love, Repeat* is a breath of fresh air. . . . Faith-filled inspiration and practical ideas for living alert, taking notice of others, and scattering God's kindness in an often negative world.

—Candace Cameron Bure, *New York
Times* bestselling author, actress,
and cohost of *The View*

In *Listen, Love, Repeat* Karen Ehman again strikes gold, showing us how to value others above ourselves and to do so with genuine compassion. A teacher at heart, Karen skillfully weaves together biblical examples, hard-earned wisdom, and real-life stories to create a resource our world desperately needs.

—Liz Curtis Higgs, bestselling author
of *The Girl's Still Got It*

Listen, Love, Repeat is utterly refreshing. It's a call to step out of our self-obsessed culture and notice the people around us, to really pay attention and look for ways to love and honor each other. What a timely reminder that while we can't do everything for the people we encounter in the day-to-day, we can do something—and every little something matters. Thank you, Karen, for a book that's practical, encouraging, and grounded in Truth. We will all be better for reading it.

—Sophie Hudson, popular blogger
BooMama, author of *Giddy Up, Eunice*
and *Home Is Where My People Are*

In *Listen, Love Repeat* Karen reminds us the purpose of doing good isn't about being known as a pretty good person but about pointing people to the breathtaking goodness of God. You won't feel like you're being asked to add one more thing to your already full plate. Instead, you'll discover how small sacrifices can have a significant impact on the lives of others. And how you can do it all for the glory of the One who made the greatest sacrifice of all.

—**Jeannie Cunnion**, author of *Parenting
the Wholehearted Child*

Listen, Love, Repeat was an answer to prayer! It's so easy to live focused on our own needs, but as I asked the Lord to show me ways to better love those around me, Karen's words inspired and equipped me to live with a heart of hospitality. This book is full of wonderful ways to live a life that reaches out and welcomes others in.

—**Becky Thompson**, author of
Hope Unfolding, founder
of Scissortail SILK

If you desire to bless others but feel like your calendar is too busy, this book is for you! *Listen, Love, Repeat* is exactly the inspiration I need to remind me that it doesn't always take a lot of time to be a blessing. Karen Ehman shows us that when we pay attention and listen to the people around us, God reveals many simple ways we can love them well. Her biblical insight, practical ideas, and creative tips will help you live the life of love you long for.

—**Courtney Joseph**, author and blogger
at WomenLivingWell.org and
GoodMorningGirls.org

With uncommon wit and wisdom, Karen Ehman shows us how to listen between the lines in everyday conversations and to love with creativity! Each chapter inspired me to live more alert and become more aware of how I can shift my focus from what people have to what they really need!

—**Renee Swope**, bestselling author
of *A Confident Heart*

Human connection is seemingly more accessible than ever, but still our hearts often feel miles away from the human being living even right next door. In *Listen, Love, Repeat* Karen Ehman digs into how meaningful connection begins by tuning our ears toward the hearts of those around us. When we do, life becomes richer and love becomes deeper. This is a practical and encouraging manual to forming and deepening relationships all around you.

—**Logan Wolfram**, speaker, author
of *Curious Faith: Rediscovering
Hope in the God of Possibility*

Listen, Love, Repeat is a go-to manual on loving others like Jesus did. Karen's heartfelt stories, biblical examples, and doable ideas will empower you to live alert–being on the lookout for anyone who needs a healthy dose of encouragement wrapped in a blanket of grace. I can't wait to implement some of the suggestions!

—**Courtney DeFeo**, speaker, author of
In This House, We Will Giggle, and
founder of Light 'Em Up Gifts

Listen, Love, Repeat is more than a book. It is an inspired call to action for Christians to do what Jesus calls us to do: love people. By the end of the first chapter, I was already looking for ways to scatter kindness. This book is more than a recitation of why our good deeds matter. It is a practical guidebook on how to be like Jesus in a world that desperately needs more kindness.

—**Jennifer Dukes Lee**, author of
The Happiness Dare

Packed with heartfelt truths and practical ideas, Karen Ehman hits the nail on the head with her newest book, *Listen, Love, Repeat*! Both challenging and inspiring, it is a message we desperately need in our world today: to love others. A must read!

—**Ruth Schwenk**, coauthor of
For Better or For Kids, founder
of TheBetterMom.com

The woman who wrote this book is the same woman who threw my bridal shower, loves me in ways I don't deserve, believes in me in ways I don't believe in myself, and gives gifts better than anyone I know. *Listen, Love, Repeat* isn't merely a catchy title, it's the way Karen Ehman lives. She hasn't stopped this cycle ever since I've met her. Now, it's your turn to start.

—**Lindsey Feldpausch**, blogger at
The Glorious Table and Karen
Ehman's real-life friend

Karen Ehman is God's real deal—her heartfelt words a gift. When I began to tear up by page fifteen, I knew my heart was in for a total transformation! *Listen, Love, Repeat* quite possibly could be the key to getting unstuck from feeling hopelessly dry, scarily empty, and completely unfulfilled. Thank you, Karen, for being the friend we need to encourage us to tune our ears—in the midst of our culture's narcissism—to hear God's heart and scatter his loved to the world.

—**Sheila Mangum**, author of the
popular prayer blog *The Power
of the Three Stranded Prayer* and
Karen Ehman's real-life friend

Listen, Love, Repeat is written by the woman I like to call my "other mother." I spend lots of time at her house. She is never too busy to listen to my struggles, feed me good food, and let me borrow her phone charger. Best of all, she's always pushing me to do my best and to strengthen my walk with the Lord. This book will help you to love like Jesus did and to never let others around you go unnoticed—even if that person is a teenage boy with a big appetite and dead cell phone who just needs someone to listen and care.

—**Anthen Ruhf**, nineteen-year-old
"sorta son" of Karen Ehman

Listen

LOVE

REPEAT

OTHER-CENTERED LIVING
IN A SELF-CENTERED WORLD

KAREN EHMAN

ZONDERVAN®

ZONDERVAN

Listen, Love, Repeat
Copyright © 2016 by Karen Ehman

Requests for information should be addressed to:
Zondervan, *3900 Sparks Dr. SE, Grand Rapids, Michigan 49546*

ISBN 978-0-310-33967-0 (softcover)

ISBN 978-0-310-34983-9 (audio)

ISBN 978-0-310-33968-7 (ebook)

Published in association with the literary agency of The FEDD Agency, Post Office Box 341973, Austin, TX 78734.

Art direction: Brian Bobel
Interior design: Denise Froehlich

First printing September 2016 / Printed in the United States of America

To my mother, Margaret Sanders Patterson,
and my daughter, Mackenzie Leith Ehman.
One who modeled for me how to listen and love.
The other who is just like her grandma.

Contents

Acknowledgments

To my Proverbs 31 Ministries sisters (and one brother!), especially President Lysa TerKeurst: Serving God with you is my favorite thing to do! I love you all.

To agent Esther Fedorkevich: Thank you for your encouragement to put together this idea about scattering kindness.

To my Harper Collins Christian family: Sandy Vander Zicht, Tom Dean, Robin Phillips, John Raymond, TJ Rathbun, and Greg Clouse. Thank you for all you do to get my projects from scribbles on a legal pad to a book and video Bible study in the hands of a woman who needs it. You all are so gifted and gracious.

To Lori Vandenbosch: Thanks for helping my words to make sense and to make a difference.

To my prayer wall—four faith-filled friends who daily pound heaven's doors for my sake: Kim Cordes, Sharon Glasgow, Mary Steinke, and Lindsey Feldpausch. I love you all.

To my husband, Todd, and kids Kenna, Mitchell, and Spencer: Being a family with you all is a delightful mixture of chaos and love.

To my Lord and Savior Jesus Christ: For dying on the cross for me, purchasing my way to heaven. Indescribable.

CHAPTER 1

Living Alert

HOW TO HEAR A HEART DROP

Do not waste time bothering whether you "love" your neighbor; act as if you did. As soon as we do this we find one of the great secrets. When you are behaving as if you loved someone, you will presently come to love him.

—C. S. LEWIS

The hearts of the people cry out to the Lord.
—LAMENTATIONS 2:18

I sat cross-legged on the floor in my friend Trisha's living room that rainy April evening, trying to balance my cup of coffee while also keeping her dog from jumping on me. My excitement had been building for weeks, and now I was finally close to the moment I had so looked forward to: my friend opening the birthday gift I'd purchased for her.

While I always love giving gifts and bringing happiness to others, this gift was special. It wasn't just something I picked up on an excursion to the department store, nor was it a gift card to her favorite restaurant. This gift was the response to a heart drop.

Let me back up and explain.

Trisha and I had been friends for over a decade. We attended the same church. Volunteered for the same organization. Our boys all played baseball up at the local Little League fields where we had numerous occasions to sit and visit in our lawn chairs under the Michigan spring skies.

During the time we spent in each other's company, we discussed many things. Mostly we talked about our children. But every once in a while we would reminisce about what it was like when we were kids growing up. We were born the same year and graduated high school at the same time. So naturally, we had many common memories of being teenagers in the 1980s. Big hair. Roller-skating. Tab soda. "Who shot JR?" Bonne Bell Lip Smackers. You get the picture.

One day when Trisha and I were at her house working on a volunteer project, the subject of school came up. I had a child who was struggling with reading. She had a child who had challenges in a different subject. As we discussed our dilemmas, we talked about our own student experiences. It was then that I discovered my friend also had struggled with reading when she was younger.

"I absolutely hated reading out loud at school," she confessed. "Because reading did not come easily to me, I was placed in the slow reading group. I had friends who could whip through books quickly, but I had trouble just keeping up with the reading I had to do for school. I didn't even like going to the library because I couldn't find any books that I could read the whole way through. All of them were filled with words I could not read."

I empathized with my friend, knowing all too well the battles of people with reading disabilities. My husband and one of my sons have dyslexia, and they had experienced the frustrations I heard Trisha express. But Trisha's face brightened as she recalled a small victory.

"There was one book I actually could read from cover to cover. It was a book my grandmother had at her house. It was chunky and square with a hard cover, and it was called *Mary Lee and the Mystery of the Indian Beads*. It sat on my grandmother's shelf, and every time I went to her house, I pulled it out and curled up on the sofa and read the whole thing from front to back. There wasn't a single word in there that I did not know. Oh, how I loved the feeling I got from reading that book!"

Trisha's telling of that story was more than just a window into her past. It was a heart drop.

A heart drop is a concept my husband and I learned from our small group leader, Michael. It's when a person, either directly or in a cryptic way, gives you a peek into his or her heart. It may be through actual words, or you may pick up on a feeling, perhaps sadness or loneliness. In the case of my conversation with Trisha, her heart surfaced as she talked about a time in her life when she felt significant, safe, and no longer inferior to the rest of the kids. At that moment her heart expressed through her words a tender and raw emotion. A longing for someone to understand, for someone to say, "I'm listening. I hear you."

I picked up on Trisha's heart drop that day. In fact, over the next week I couldn't get that story out of my head. I knew her birthday was coming up in April, so one evening, I decided to see if I could track down this antique book. I knew it might be like looking for a lost Lego in the bottom of a toy box, but I was determined to try anyway.

I logged onto my eBay account, did a quick search, and there it was: an image of a vintage copy of *Mary Lee and the Mystery of the Indian Beads* by Alice Andersen, copyright 1937. I checked the time the auction would be ending: not until after midnight. A few other people were already bidding on the book, so I set my alarm for fifteen minutes before the auction's end.

When the alarm went off, I dragged myself to the basement and logged on to my computer. The bids had not gone up by much. I calculated the top price I was willing to pay and entered it. But then I waited until only about a minute and a half remained before the auction's end to register my bid. When I hit "send," the wonderful words popped up on the screen: "You are the top bidder." I was thrilled! I kept refreshing my screen until the auction ended. I had won the book! I could hardly wait to wrap it up and give it to my friend.

When Trisha opened her gift that night in her living room, she could scarcely believe her eyes. Of course she was astonished that she now held in her hands a retro copy of this beloved book. What floored her even more was the fact that somehow I knew she would love it. She looked up at me with such excitement in her eyes. "Wait! But how did you know?" she exclaimed.

I reminded her of our conversation months earlier about her struggle with reading and the respite she found at her grandmother's house while reading this treasured book. Although the conversation had been a heart drop at the time, she didn't recall it taking place. And she certainly couldn't believe that I remembered and then acted upon it.

Hearing a heart drop is an art we must lovingly cultivate. It can lead to the most wonderful times of encouragement as we make it our habit to listen and to love.

—— Seduced by Selfie-Centered Living ——

Our culture is obsessed with self. We post pictures of ourselves online. What we're eating. What we're doing. We're focused on *our* schedules, *our* relationships. At every turn we seem to care about only one thing: "What's in it for me?"

We are so saturated with self, it begins to seem almost normal. Expected. Even embraced. As a result, many of the old-fashioned virtues seem to have disappeared. Holding the door open for someone. Saying, "No, after you," not only with our words but with our actions. Looking out for others. Giving a helping hand. Such other-centered behaviors are as scarce as a modern home with a rotary phone. Perhaps our busyness is partly to blame. We race from one activity to the next. The demands of work and family—not to mention volunteer commitments—clamor for our attention. Although we may interact with others daily as we carry out our responsibilities, rarely do we pay attention to what is really going on in the lives of those around us.

Because near-narcissism and the too-busy lifestyle is the normal default, to become a person who thinks of others first takes great effort on our part. It requires us to live alert. To be on the lookout not only for conversational heart drops but for those who might need a helping hand or a dose of encouragement—with no expectation of a return favor. In other words, with no strings attached.

Over the years I have been blessed to know a few people who lived like this. Their attentiveness to the emotional and physical needs of others, coupled with their loving actions, and often accompanying creative ideas, have made a deep impression on me.

First and foremost, I think of my own mother. She was well known for making even ordinary days special for those in her life. I remember the year she left a little gift for me on the table for when I returned home from cheerleading tryouts, along with a clever poem. She had a knack for coming up with the perfect presents, often due to her own keen ability to hear a heart drop. She was also known for gifts—and pranks—of silliness. I still remember the black, rotten banana she and her friend from work gave back and forth to each other for birthdays over the course of nearly a decade. I never did know the whole story behind the crazy (and fruity!) tradition, only that she and her friend got a huge kick out of it twice a year.

Others in my life have also modeled putting others first. You will meet some of them on the pages of this book. You will also meet souls from the pages of Scripture who did the same thing. But the greatest model of all for living alert is the Lord Jesus himself.

WDJD (What Did Jesus Do)

I never tire of reading the Gospel accounts of Jesus' life. Although I love reading from both the Old and New Testaments and have attempted some of those "Bible in a Year" plans (aka "The Start-Out-All-Spiritual-and-Fizzle-by-February Plan"), I would be perfectly happy just to sit and soak in the Scriptures that give eyewitness account to what Jesus did when he was on Earth. The Gospels make Jesus come to life in HD. (Wouldn't that be the best reality show of all?)

Although he was the Son of God and on a very big mission, Jesus was never too busy to notice. He lived alert. He could be among a crowd of thousands and yet focus in on one weary soul who needed a look, a word, or a touch from him. Sometimes, even while on his way to do something that seemed grander and more important, he turned his attention to what appeared to be lesser requests. Because Jesus wasn't about doing *big things*. He was about doing the *right thing*. And often for him, the right thing was noticing one simple soul.

Luke 8 and Mark 5 both record such a scene for us. Christ had just restored a demon-possessed man. That was surely something grand! Then he crossed over to the other side of the lake with his disciples. A large crowd soon gathered. A ruler of the synagogue named Jairus was among the people who wanted to see Jesus, and he had a rather desperate request. His daughter was dying and he longed for Jesus to come and heal her. Jesus agreed. There wasn't a lot of hoopla surrounding his decision. He didn't draw attention to what he was about to go do—posting it on Twitter with the hashtag #miracleontheway, or uploading a pic on Instagram with a really cool filter for effect. We are simply told in Mark 5:24, "So Jesus went with him."

As they journeyed to the place where Jairus's beloved daughter lay dying, crowds once again pressed in all around Jesus. In the throng was a woman. The Bible says of her,

> She had suffered a great deal under the care of many doctors and had spent all she had, yet instead of getting better she grew worse. When she heard about Jesus, she came up behind him in the crowd and touched his cloak, because she thought, "If I just touch his clothes, I will be healed." (Mark 5:26–28)

And so she reached out to touch Jesus—she and multitudes of others who also were reaching for the Savior. But her simple, frantic touch didn't escape his notice.

> At once Jesus realized that power had gone out from him. He turned around in the crowd and asked, "Who touched my clothes?" "You see the people crowding

against you," his disciples answered, "and yet you can ask, 'Who touched me?'" (vv. 30–31)

Trembling, the woman admitted it was she. Jesus responded, "Daughter, your faith has healed you. Go in peace and be freed from your suffering" (v. 34).

This story has always fascinated me. The way Jesus took time—while in the middle of a crowd of people—to notice just one person and meet her need. The need of a seemingly insignificant person. She wasn't important like the synagogue ruler Jairus. In fact, we aren't even told her name. Yet she was not unimportant to Jesus.

Jairus became worried that this little side tour had taken up too much time, and perhaps now it was too late for his daughter. But it is never too late for Jesus. He still journeyed on to heal Jairus's daughter as well.

Could we try to be more like Jesus, this perfect man who was never too busy to notice someone who needed his touch? Sure, we also have many things calling for our attention. Crowds of people and projects press in. Whether at work or at home, we are often on our way to do something grand. But Jesus is calling us to stop and notice. To live alert. To give a special touch that may heal a heart or cheer a weary soul.

I once heard it said that Jesus' real ministry was the person he found standing in front of him. Who is that for *you* today? Rather than trying to do something grand for God, perhaps we need to embrace the obscure instead. To stop trying to be profound or important and instead just be obedient. To quickly and humbly obey when we feel God calling us to engage with another or to cheer and hearten a weary soul. Are you willing to mimic the behavior of Jesus?

People all around us every day are longing for someone to notice them. They may feel alone or ashamed. Afraid or apprehensive. The simple act of noticing someone as he or she journeys through life can lovingly mirror the behavior of God. But in order to behave like Jesus did, and spread the healing balm of his love, we must be willing to drop our agenda—or at least put it on hold—to reach out and touch those who need it most. The scene doesn't have to be impressive. The circumstances are usually quite ordinary. And often the stage is set right in front of us as we go about our days. In fact, sometimes the stage is set right within our own four walls.

My Magnetic Kitchen Island

I remember when my husband and I were searching for a home to purchase. Everyone in our family had their opinion about the must-haves for our new home. My daughter wanted a bedroom with a large closet so she could organize her purses, shoes, and other teenage apparel. One son wanted a sprawling backyard—one spacious enough to host a rousing game of flag football for all his friends. Still another son hoped for a hot tub. (Oh well . . . a guy can dream, can't he?) My husband—ever the practical and frugal guy—wanted a house with low property taxes. But I had a different desire. I wanted a kitchen island. I was thrilled when we found a house in our price range with that very feature. And so seven years ago we moved into the little brick house with the big kitchen island. And that island quickly became a popular attraction.

Yes, my kitchen island is a hoppin' place. While I would love for it to be HGTV-like, adorned with a beautiful bouquet of flowers and an antique bowl of colorful fruits, most often this is not the case. Instead, the island is a catchall. Stray school papers, unpaid bills, and pizza coupons seem to find their way there. Sacks of groceries wait there to be put away.

But papers, cans, and cartons aren't the only constant callers. My island is also a people magnet. Family members gather there for a quick sandwich or reheated leftovers on their way to and from school and work. I share a cup of coffee with a friend there during a break in a busy day. My children's friends pull up a stool and inquire, "Mama Karen, what ya got that's good to eat?" My island seems to draw people in, inviting them to sit for a spell, even among the clutter.

The greatest magnetic pull occurs during times of celebration—formal holidays as well as spur-of-the-moment, unofficial gatherings. At Christmas and Easter, the island pulls double duty as a buffet bar, showcasing Uncle Kevin's barbecued meatballs, Grandma Margaret's fancified veggie tray, Aunt Loraine's melt-in-your-mouth fudge. But it's the impromptu everyday moments we celebrate around my kitchen island that I treasure most: A completed English paper. A chemistry concept finally understood. Braces coming off. A successful football season (our team won the state championship this year—our fifth in six seasons, just in case you were wondering!). Simple celebrations.

Over the years these impromptu gatherings have drawn a diverse group of people into our lives and created lasting memories. But more importantly, these get-togethers have been a perfect time for me to learn to live alert—in other words, to practice my faith.

We sometimes make our faith so complicated. It's true we should seek to understand deep theological truths. But there are also many simple commands tucked in the pages of Scripture about how to love others well. Most books of the Bible are a beautiful blend of both.

Hebrews 13 is a perfect example of this. It gives us a glimpse into the type of sacrifices that please God: hospitality, entertaining angels, treating our spouses properly, honoring leaders, keeping away from false teaching, and other important issues that affected the early church and are still relevant to us today.

And then, softly woven through some theological thoughts, we read this: "Through Jesus, therefore, let us continually offer to God a sacrifice of praise—the fruit of lips that openly profess his name. And do not forget to do good and to share with others, for with such sacrifices God is pleased" (Hebrews 13:15–16).

I see in this verse three simple ways to spread love:

1. Praise God by professing his name with our lips.
2. Do good.
3. Share with others.

And what is the result of our performing these straightforward actions? Pleasing God.

As loved ones, friends, and even strangers gather around us—at a cozy kitchen island, in a crowded coffee house, or in an office cubicle—this verse can be a template for us to have ever on our minds, along with its three directives.

We can look for natural—not forced or contrived—opportunities to speak of God and his goodness.

We can try to do good: Assist a teenager with his homework. Fix a broken strap on another's backpack. Help a young woman sort out a difficult relationship. Encourage a timid coworker or cheer up a weary neighbor.

And we can share. Our home. Our food—no matter how humble and un-gourmet. Our dishes (that sometimes get chipped or broken). Our time. Our heart. Our faith.

I smile when I think of how such small "sacrifices" done in Jesus' name please God. And while cooking, cleaning, and exposing your dishes to potential damage might seem like an inconvenience at first—yes, even a sacrifice—these actions not only please God, but they can bring us pleasure as well. So can spending our time with others outside of our four walls—taking them out for lunch or even a simple cup of coffee. Pausing. Listening. Loving.

Opening our lives to sacrificially celebrate holidays, holy days, and the everyday gives us opportunities to serve. It beckons us to be others-centered. Such serving brings us joy, produces fond memories, and creates lasting, soul-to-soul connections. Showing love can be the avenue God uses for someone to begin a relationship with him—due in part to our words, deeds, and shared possessions.

How might the Holy Spirit be tapping on your heart today, prompting you to praise God, do good, and share life? Your very presence and prayerful attitude can be a magnet that draws other souls to you and points them straight toward him.

Ordinary Holiness

I attended a funeral recently for my close friend Debi's dad. Few people look forward to attending funerals. The sadness, the loss, the reality that they can no longer be with their loved one.

This funeral, however, was filled with moments of ordinary holiness. I witnessed, through the pictures, the presentation, and the words of those left behind, a man who loved his friends, his community, his family, and his God. A man who knew how to hear a heart drop. And not just hear it, but respond.

Mr. H's funeral was an inspiration to me. I came home determining that, if I ever do grow up, I want to be just like him. The medals and honors (from military service, Kiwanis, and community), the gleam in his eye for his wife of six decades, the commitment to raise his kids in the way God instructs, the doting he did on his grandkids and great-granddaughter. The entire service spoke volumes of his simple, servant's heart. But what hit me the most was that he did so much secretly. I wouldn't call him a "quiet" man, for he always had a joke or witty comment whenever I greeted him.

But he gave quietly.

One by one, stories emerged of the times he, unselfishly and without recognition, gave. Sometimes it was shoveling a neighbor's driveway without being asked. Or taking them hot baked muffins. Another time it was quietly paying a church's tax bill of $1,000—a church he didn't even attend. Yet another story of the time when, each week for an entire year, he tucked a $100 bill into a struggling family's mailbox, expecting no repayment except for the joy of knowing he was giving because God told him to.

Mr. H also was probably the most loyal husband I knew. He stayed hopelessly and visibly in love with his dear wife of sixty-two years, caring for her quietly and lovingly through more than fifty of those years when her medical condition required countless hospital trips and stays, caring for his children alone during those times, and then administering home care for her in her later years, often around the clock.

He never complained. He counted it a sincere joy to serve his sweet wife.

Amazing.

As I sat there weeping, I was struck by the holy moments this man created in the seemingly mundane days of his life.

So often we want thrill, excitement, recognition, purpose. Mr. H found purpose quietly serving the person standing in front of him. With an audience of only One.

Now he is with that One forever, no doubt hearing the words of Jesus, "Well done, thou good and faithful servant . . . enter thou into the joy of thy lord" (Matthew 25:21 KJV). Yes, through the nearly quarter century that I knew my friend's father, whenever I looked at him, I sort of saw him.

But mostly, I saw Jesus.

Oh, that we all would learn to live and leave such a legacy!

The Two Reasons We Are on Earth

When I first became a Christian as a teenager, my spiritual mother told me that we are on Earth for only two reasons. The first is to have a relationship with God, our loving Creator, who offers us a place in heaven. The second is to take every opportunity we can to point others to Jesus so they can spend eternity in heaven too.

Because really—even though I know it sounds cliché—we can't take anything with us when we die. Why do we spend so much time trying to amass wealth in order to purchase houses or cars or pretty clothes when we will leave all those things behind? As the song my boot-wearing, countrified son was listening to in the car the other day says: "I've never seen a hearse with a trailer hitch."

In other words, we don't do good for the sake of looking good; we do good in order to point others to Jesus.

> "You are the light of the world. A town built on a hill cannot be hidden. Neither do people light a lamp and put it under a bowl. Instead they put it on its stand, and it gives light to everyone in the house. In the same way, let your light shine before others, that they

may see your good deeds and glorify your Father in heaven." (Matthew 5:14–16)

Don't do good works in order to selfishly shout, "Look at me!" Do them in order to humbly implore, "Will you look at *him*?"

Are you ready to fight against our selfie-obsessed culture? To stop putting self first and instead think about others? To live alert, and tune your ears to hear a heart drop?

I have come to believe this upside-down truth: if you want to find your life, first you need to lose it. In order to bring joy to yourself, first you need to be more concerned with bringing joy to others. If you want to feel significant, you need to embrace obscurity and instead make others feel significant.

Only when we love and share and serve, as Scripture commands us, can we live life on purpose, embracing the reason God brought us to Earth in the first place. As we reach out not only to friends and family but to strangers, the lonely, and the less-than-lovely, we will learn to mirror Christ and to let his light shine so that he gets all the glory.

Tuning Your Ears

So how exactly do we live alert, tuning our ears so we can hear the heart drops of those around us?

First, we need to pray and ask Jesus for a humble, servant's heart.

Second, we need to use alone time for preparation. Prayer and Bible reading tune the heart to the Spirit's movements and where he would have us act. Sleep, exercise, and healthful eating keep the mind sharp and the body ready for use. A clean(ish) home and (mostly) sane schedule allow for both interruption and reflection, two components of tuned ears.

Third, we need to live with eyes and ears wide open. No dull shuffling through the duties of life. No sleepwalking through our schedule.

Fourth, we need to focus on the face in front of us. The email in our inbox. The appointment on our calendar. The name that rises unbidden in our thoughts. Even the all-too-familiar form that sits and sleeps near us every day. What are they thinking? What are they feeling? Can you climb behind their eyeballs and see the world from their eyes, if only for a moment?

Living our lives prayerfully, preparedly, purposely, and perceptively will help us to tune our ears to the heart drops of others, so we can respond to their deepest needs in a meaningful, Spirit-centered way. On this Earth we may not even be aware of the effects of our words and actions. But we will have brought joy to the One who fills us with joy to overflowing: Jesus.

As we embark on this journey to live an other-centered life in the midst of a self-centered world, will you commit to listening, loving, and then doing it all over again? If such a way of living intrigues you, will you join me in this prayer?

Father, tune my ears to the heart drops all around me. I want to begin to live alert—to be ever on the lookout for where I might serve you by loving and serving others. Give me eyes to see the needy, ears to hear the hurting, a smile to encourage the weary, and hands ready to help those who need it. I want to be sensitive to the times you gently tap me on the heart, urging me to put love in action. May I willingly share my home, my food, my resources, and my time with whomever you send my way. When people look at me, may they instead see only you. Thank you in advance for the joy that comes from serving. In Jesus' name. Amen.

TIPS FOR LIVING ALERT

Becoming a person who hears—and responds to—a heart drop takes a little forethought and organization. Here are some ideas to help you become attentive and responsive to the spoken and unspoken emotional and physical needs of those around you.

♥ **Pray each day.** Ask God to tune your ears, focus your eyes, and soften your heart to the needs of those around you. Make this your prayer before your feet even hit the floor in the morning and your first cup of coffee splashes in your mug.

♥ **Take notes: mental ones and sticky ones.** You can do this by keeping a small notebook in your purse or utilizing the notes app on your phone. Sticky notes on your bulletin board also work well. (I love sticky notes! With the amount I buy, I should have purchased stock in the sticky notes industry!) When you hear someone mention a like or an interest, jot it down. Does your friend adore coconut? Record it. Did she mention when her birthday was? Write that down too. Did your boss tell a funny story about his favorite childhood toy or your neighbor mention which sports team she roots for? Log this info as well. Did you recently attend a funeral? Check the obituary or memorial card for the deceased's birthday and make note of it. Plan to do something for their loved ones when this day rolls around.

♥ **Pay attention to special dates.** Did your neighbor mention that he is having surgery next Tuesday? Did a teen at church talk about basketball tryouts being next week? Did a friend tell you she is expecting to hear about an offer on a new house by Monday morning? Set an alarm on your phone or record these events in your calendar. Pray for their situations, but also make an effort to get back with these people to ask them what the results were. It will mean so much to them that you remembered and followed up with them!

♥ **Start stalking.** Check out their Facebook, Twitter, or Instagram accounts. Often here you can see patterns. You will discover the likes—and even sometimes obsessions—of your friends, family, and coworkers. From their online interactions you will get ideas for ways to encourage and surprise them as well.

♥ **Be a smart shopper.** Stock an arsenal of affection, stock-piling items that will be useful as you share love with others. Be on the lookout not only for the items you have recorded from listening but also generic items such as note cards, scented candles, lotions, simple pieces of jewelry, journals, pretty pens, or fancy chocolates—all items that you can present as a simple "I was thinking of you" gift on a random day.

CHAPTER 2

Find Your Why

PSSST... IT'S ALL ABOUT RELATIONSHIPS!

Piglet sidled up to Pooh from behind. "Pooh!" he whispered. "Yes, Piglet?" "Nothing," said Piglet, taking Pooh's paw. "I just wanted to be sure of you."

—A. A. MILNE

No one has ever seen God; but if we love one another, God lives in us and his love is made complete in us.

—1 JOHN 4:12

I grabbed my canvas book bag, slung it over my shoulder, and headed out of my dormitory to trudge across campus to the library, where a few students and I were gathering that windy autumn afternoon to work on our assignment for Philosophy 200. (I may have had an extra spring in my step because a cute new student named Todd Ehman would be there—and I might have a chance to sit next to him!) The project that day included thinking through and coming up with what the professor in our small Christian college called our *summum bonum*.

Summum bonum is a Latin expression meaning "the highest good." It was introduced by Cicero to parallel the "Idea of the Good" in ancient Greek philosophy. The *summum bonum* is commonly referred to as an end in itself that also encompasses all other goods in life. In medieval times the phrase was used to describe the act of ultimate importance—that singular and paramount pursuit that human beings should strive to do.

Our professor gave us several examples of what someone might choose as their highest good in life. Perhaps it was God. Or family. Or caring for the poor. There really was no correct answer. It was up to us to prayerfully consider the assignment and then present our case for what was most significant to each of us and why, gathering in small groups to explain our choice.

As I sat in the library fiddling with my number two pencil, I tried to think of what I would choose as my *summum bonum* to share with the group. What was most important to me in life? What did I think was the highest good—the chief pursuit that mattered more than anything else?

I decided I would choose relationships.

Even at my young age I had already heard many people say how when we pass away, we cannot take anything with us. And I remembered my spiritual mother's assertion that the only two reasons we are on Earth are to have a relationship with God and to show others the way of salvation through Jesus. Their comments showed me that things were less important than people. Certainly what was most precious to me were my family, my close friends, and my fellow brothers and sisters at the church I'd attended in the three years I had been a believer. It wasn't hard for me to write a paper asserting that what mattered most in life is relationships. So I whipped out a canary-yellow legal pad and began to scratch out my thesis and main points, determined to make the argument that nothing in life mattered more than people. *Nothing.*

That philosophy assignment was decades ago, but I still believe that nothing in life matters more than relationships. And the longer I am on this Earth, the more convinced I am that it's true.

Why Am I Here?

One of the oldest questions known to humans might very well be, "Why am I here?" Something deep within us longs to know the meaning of life. Is there a point to it? And if so, what is it? Where do I fit in the grand scheme of things? And if I am on Earth for a purpose, how do I find it? We simply do not want to go through life having missed our cause and calling.

Pastor Rick Warren tackled this topic in his bestselling book *The Purpose Driven Life*, subtitled *What on Earth Am I Here For?* In just the first five years after the book released, it sold over thirty million copies. Thirty million people wanted to know their purpose for being on Earth!

Warren's book was his attempt to lay out the biblical perspective on why we exist. Society, of course, has its own answers to this question. One answer is to grab all the gusto we can. After all, we only go around once, right? We might as well live it up and accumulate all of the material possessions or memorable experiences that we can. Just look at some of the popular hashtags in social media. #yolo stands for "you only live once." People use this phrase to justify some of their outlandish or crazy behavior. (Perhaps even some illegal behavior as well!) And #fomo reminds us of our "fear of missing out." After all, we don't want to be left behind.

Interestingly, for all of social media's frequent illustrations of people's narcissism and selfishness, it also gives us glimpses of true acts of kindness and episodes of thoughtfulness. The articles, pictures, and videos associated with such benevolent behaviors often go viral. Just today I saw the following stories trending on social media:

- ♥ A police officer who used his own money to buy a homeless family clothes, food, and a ten-night stay in a local hotel

- ♥ A social worker who decided to adopt one of her clients, a teenager who had been in foster care for over a decade

- ♥ A customer who gave a four-digit tip to a faithful waitress so she could pay down some of her college debt

While many of us may be self-centered and care too much about material possessions or glamorous experiences, we also celebrate selfless acts of kindness and care for other humans. (And animals. I mean, who doesn't love a great animal rescue story!)

What does this tell us? Perhaps we all experience a tension between the selfishness of what we want to do and the appeal of the truly heartwarming and touching stories of kindness we see. We long to live unselfishly as well, but sometimes we are just too accustomed to our self-centered living. Or we think that our small acts of kindness don't add up to much, while the grand ones we spy online seem to make a real difference. Or maybe we have just been conditioned from birth to think of ourselves first; our default mode is to look out for number one. Perhaps if we paid closer attention to why our hearts are drawn to such stories, we'd discover it is because we are called not only to view them online but to live them out in our own lives as well!

A Three-Step Life Plan

Of course Jesus gave us the answer not only to *why* we are here but *what* we are supposed to do while we're here. Take a look at how he answered a tough question a religious leader asked him, and what his answer teaches us about our *why* and our *what*:

> "Teacher, which is the greatest commandment in the Law?" Jesus replied: "'Love the Lord your God with all your heart and with all your soul and with all your mind.' This is the first and greatest commandment. And the second is like it: 'Love your neighbor as yourself.' All the Law and the Prophets hang on these two commandments." (Matthew 22:36–40)

Jesus asserts that the entire teaching of God—all the law and the prophets—hinge upon these commands, which can be summed up in this three-step life plan:

1. Love God.
2. Love others.
3. Love yourself.

Relationships. Relationships. And *more* relationships. Why are we here? To love. What are we supposed to do? Again: love. God, others, and even self.

When I became a Christian, I read the command to love yourself and thought it was strange. I thought surely the Christian thing to do was to think very little of ourselves. The concept of loving myself was very foreign. But when I followed Jesus' line of logic, I came to a different conclusion.

If Jesus told us we are to love our neighbor "as ourselves," then it must be crucial that we do indeed possess self-love. If we put ourselves down or neglect our most basic physical or emotional needs, we would not be a good model for how we are to treat our fellow human beings. Slowly my understanding of this verse began to change.

How do we love ourselves? Well, we make sure that we have enough to eat. We take care to see that we have clothes to wear. We make sure we are sheltered. We seek self-respect and safety, security, and significance. We nurture our important relationships. And then we realize that these are the same things we should make sure our neighbor has. When we love ourselves, we can see that God calls us to love others in the same way.

Still, it can be difficult to strike a balance. Sometimes we think too little of ourselves. Other times we may think of ourselves too much, leaving very little time to reach out and to love others. How can we properly address both problems at the same time: the problem of self-loathing and the problem of self-love? The answer lies within the passage we have just visited. Look back at what Jesus declares is the greatest commandment of all:

> "Love the Lord your God with all your heart and with all your soul and with all your mind." (Matthew 22:37)

Learning to manage the tension between putting ourselves first and thinking of the needs of others happens when we put loving God at the very top of our "How to Live" list.

If we truly love God with our hearts and souls and minds, we will want to get to know him through the pages of Scripture. We will long to spend time with him in prayer. We will hunger to get to know his heart and mind as we seek to discover his will for our lives. And as we interact with God through prayer and experience his heart through studying the Scriptures, we will learn how to live properly. We will learn that thinking of ourselves with a proper perspective and reaching out in love to others always go together. And when we live in this manner, we will be able to maintain the purpose I learned as a young Christian: to go about our days strengthening our relationship with God as we look forward to eternity, but also being on the lookout for ways to share Christ with others so that they may spend eternity in heaven with him as well. All of this takes place within the context of relationships.

Perhaps I got my little philosophy assignment correct. Maybe relationships are the highest good in life—with others here on Earth, but most importantly with God.

Who Comes First?

Not only do we need to find the balance between loving others and loving ourselves, we also need to make daily and even minute-by-minute decisions about who to love right now. As a young mom with three children under the age of six, I had to decide whether to feed the crying baby, show attention to the wailing toddler, or help the kindergartener learn her alphabet. As a friend and church member, I need to decide if I will go to coffee with a hurting friend or help out with the annual Christmas outreach event, as I had promised. Who—or what—comes first?

That's where we need to return to Step #1: Love God. Because when you love God first, seek his will, and learn to listen for the unique way he communicates with you, he can begin to make plain your path for each day and each moment. God knows we are limited by time and space; Jesus himself was. He didn't preach to everyone, heal everyone, comfort everyone, or even convert everyone. He simply showed up where God told him to go and did what God told him to do.

Years ago I received a call from an organization inviting me to speak at their event. This was a large ministry that I'd always dreamed of speaking for, and the conference was in a part of the country I'd never visited but had always wanted to see. However, when they told me the date of the event, my heart sank. It was the same weekend as my son Mitchell's fifth birthday. Turning five was a big deal at our house because it was the first year you got to have a party with friends.

When I shared my concern with the coordinator, she suggested that I hold his party on a different weekend so I could still attend the conference. But I knew that my son would know it wasn't on his actual birthday. My heart did flip-flops in my chest as I weighed the decision. I wanted to say yes to the speaking event, but I did not want to disappoint my son or make him feel less important than my ministry. After a little thought and a lot of prayer, I regrettably declined.

The weekend of the party made it Windex clear to me that I had made the right decision. Seeing my son excitedly eating meat-lovers pizza and chocolate éclair cake with his friends—and his enthusiastic thank-you hug around the neck when the party was over—reassured me I had chosen well. Years later I smiled when I was asked to speak at the same conference, also around the time of my son's birthday. This time, though, I said yes to the organization and took Mitchell with me to the event. We had a great time together, and he was able to go backstage to meet his favorite Christian recording artist who was also appearing at the same event.

Establishing our priorities with God's guidance and then living in a way that reflects these priorities will sometimes mean making tough calls. Resolving on the front end that we will make choices that align with our priorities helps us to sort through the decision-making process. It allows us to live a life of love while keeping our most important relationships protected and healthy.

Find Me Somebody to Love

When I look at my own life, a quick survey reveals no shortage of relationships. Of course, first and foremost, I am a wife and mother. These two roles connect me to my most important relationships in life.

Beyond that, I have my extended family. I am a daughter. And a sister. And a stepdaughter. And a daughter-in-law. And a crazy aunt. I have cousins and second cousins. Aunts and uncles. By blood or by marriage, I am related to many people on this Earth.

Then there are those I know with whom I share no blood or legal relationship. My neighbors. My friends. My children's teachers. The folks at church and on the sidelines of the football field. These people are in my life on an ongoing basis. Some of them I chose. Others I was assigned.

And then there are those I affectionately refer to as "necessary people," those individuals who enable me to live life. The mail carrier. Our doctor. The woman behind the dry cleaner's counter and the man bagging my groceries. The garbage collector. While these people may seem to have been randomly thrust into my day, I believe they are there on purpose. And I believe that God's admonishment to me to love others also applies to them. (More on those relationships in chapter four!)

Finally, there are strangers, those men and women whom I may know only for a brief moment. What do my actions say to them? Might any of my encounters with these people be designed by God on purpose to either teach me a lesson or to show them love? Perhaps it is the grandfather sitting next to me at the game. Or the frazzled mom in the grocery store trying to wrestle one of her children back into the shopping cart. Maybe even the agitated and in-a-hurry woman who cuts me off in traffic. Could I treat my encounters with them in a way that shows kindness? Can I ask the grandfather about his grandson? Could I lend a helping hand to that frustrated mom? Could I go so far as to reply to the angry driver's gestures with a smile instead of a curse?

Our relationships give us an opportunity to show God's love to others. In our narcissistic and self-absorbed culture, other-centered behavior stands out. Way out.

"One Another" Commands

Scripture has a lot to say about how we should treat each other. In fact, the New Testament contains nearly forty verses of relational instructions, all containing the telling phrase "one another." These "one another" commands in Scripture tell us how we are or are not to treat each other! Scripture is serious about relationships and how they are to play out.

Let's peruse a few of these "one another" verses (I've included all of them at the end of the chapter). The first one is spoken by Jesus himself.

> "A new command I give you: Love *one another*. As I have loved you, so you must love *one another*. By this everyone will know that you are my disciples, if you

love *one another.*" (John 13:34–35, emphasis added here and following)

Jesus is the model for love. His love is sacrificial. Consistent. Unconditional. Without strings attached. We accurately model for others the love of Christ toward us when we seek to love them in the same way. The people in our life can catch a glimpse of God when they see us seeking to mirror his love.

On to another verse:

> Be devoted to *one another* in love. Honor *one another* above yourselves. (Romans 12:10)

So often we forget that relationships aren't easy. They require loyalty and steadfast devotion. Sometimes marriages dissolve because feelings fade. We give up on friendships when they get hard. We decide that our children have so severely disappointed us as adults that we let our relationships with them dwindle as well. But the commands to us in this portion of Romans are clear: *Don't hang up on your relationships; hang in there instead.*

This verse also tells us to honor others above ourselves. What does this look like? It isn't just taking the smallest piece of coconut cream pie left in the pan, leaving the bigger ones for others. It isn't just holding a door for someone or letting a waiting car in at a crowded intersection. Honoring others means thinking of their desires, wishes, and welfare at those times you want to put yourself first. It is trusting God as you let go of what you feel is your right to be right. It is speaking kindly and respectfully. Showing deference at times and lifting others up always. As we honor others, we reflect Jesus. As Paul reminded us:

> In your relationships with *one another*, have the same mindset as Christ Jesus: Who, being in very nature God, did not consider equality with God something to be used to his own advantage; rather, he made himself nothing by taking the very nature of a servant, being made in human likeness. And being found in appearance as a man, he humbled himself by becoming obedient to death—even death on a cross! (Philippians 2:5–8)

If Jesus himself put others first, then—even though at times it is oh-so-challenging—we can strive to do so as well!

Finally, a little further in Romans we read this:

> Rejoice with those who rejoice; mourn with those who mourn. Live in harmony with *one another*. Do not be proud, but be willing to associate with people of low position. Do not be conceited. (Romans 12:15–16)

Weeping. Rejoicing. Associating. Living humbly in harmony with others. Jesus modeled these behaviors for us. He knew his call included both joy and sorrow. He knew he didn't come to Earth to hang around the popular and pretty people but to reach the outcast. To include the marginalized. To notice those who least expect to be noticed. This was right in God's eyes. And it still is right for us today.

Loving others includes not just giving of our time but feeling with our hearts as well.

We must be willing not only to associate ourselves with others, but also to feel their pain and share their joy. We must mingle our tears with theirs, raise our laughter in harmonious chorus with theirs, and thereby mimic Christ and reflect his love.

If our perspective each day can be "I am in it for you" instead of "What is in it for me?" we will discover the joy of serving Jesus—without expecting anything in return and done only for an audience of One. We may show this kind of love to family or friends. Or we might demonstrate it in a random encounter with a stranger. Either way, the stage is set for us to showcase God's love to a watching world.

On Lumping and Loving

I usually cringe at generalizations . . . stereotypes. I hate lumping an entire group of people into a confining box. Like "The _____ (nationality) are so _____ (bad character trait)" or "Those _____ (age group) all are so _____ (strange habit or behavior)." Every once in a while, though, I'm glad to hear about people being lumped together.

Recently, as I waited in line at a coffeehouse, a frail, elderly woman stood in front of me ordering a meal. She seemed distressed as she fumbled for her change, paid the worker, and then gathered up her bag of food and her drink. As she headed for the door, her large purse began swinging off of her shoulder, nearly knocking her, and all of her lunch, to the floor.

"Oh . . . how am I going to do this? Oh my . . . oh dear . . . I can't . . . ," she mumbled to herself, trying to shift her weight and her cargo while pushing open the door at the same time.

Though I'd just reached the front of the line, God tapped me on the heart and shifted my momentary schedule. I quickly hopped out of line.

"Here, let me get that for you," I said as I held the door open and steadied her drink. "Would you like me to carry your food to your car?"

She stopped in her tracks, her bright blue eyes looking up at me with gratefulness. "Oh, dear . . . you must have a grandmother living that you're so kind to an old woman."

"No, ma'am, I don't," I answered. "I just love Jesus, and he wants me to help you."

Her face softened. She shook her head and decidedly declared, "Of course! You people have always been so helpful to me. I don't know what I'd do without you."

You people. I'm pretty sure she meant, "You Christians."

She didn't align herself with Christians by saying, "Thank you for helping a sister out." No, she referred to me—and others who loved Jesus—as "you people." It made me wonder, how had other Christians helped her? Did they take her a meal? Rake her yard in the fall or shovel her driveway in the winter? Had they driven her to a doctor's appointment?

It reminded me of the age-old truth: more is caught

than taught. It also demonstrated to me that people are watching. And lumping. What do they see? Do they see us being considerate in all we do?

Sadly, I have been told the following:

By a waitress: "Christians are the worst tippers, especially after a Sunday supper out. Sometimes they leave no money at all."

By an acquaintance in college: "You're a Christian? Do you stand in front of the science building and scream Bible verses, telling people they're going to hell for believing in evolution?"

By a teenager: "I tried going to church once. There was a sign on the front door that said, 'All are welcome, but please dress appropriately.' I didn't know what *appropriately* meant, but I knew it wasn't me. So I turned around and left."

By a fellow football mom on the sidelines of a game: "I can't stand these Christians online. All they ever do is throw around Bible verses and tell everyone who doesn't think exactly as they do that they are wrong. They don't seem to want to listen to the other side. They are rude. Christians are some of the meanest people I know."

If people are watching us and all they see are uncaring or condemning Christians, why oh why would they ever want to become one? My prayer is that we, as Christ-followers, will be lumped in the "you people" group my sweet coffeehouse friend saw. Considerate Christians who make God and his body of believers look good. Sure, believers already know God is good. But others?

They are watching. And lumping. What will they see in us? Will they catch a glimpse of a God who loves them? Will they see someone who pauses in their day to put others first? Or will they see just another selfish, self-absorbed person who cares little for anyone else? Will we stand out from the crowd, or will we conveniently blend in? The choice is ours.

May we purpose today to find our purpose—in serving others. All of our own unique others. The ones with whom we share a bloodline or last name. The ones we encounter daily as we go about our routines. The ones at work. Or in our neighborhoods. Yes, even the random strangers or grumpy drivers. They are on-purpose people. May we find our why in our relationships with them.

They can become our *summum bonum*—our greatest good.

Father, thank you for the relationships in my life. All of them. The ones that bring me delight. The ones that are out of duty. And even the ones that get on my very last nerve. I know that you work in the midst of relationships as we learn to give and take. To serve and love. May I be intentional today to pour into my relationships, strengthening them according to your Word. I want to live out your command to "live in harmony with one another." May I do it all to your glory. In Jesus' name. Amen.

39 "ONE ANOTHERS" IN THE NEW TESTAMENT

Our relationships with "one another" matter. Here are thirty-nine passages from the New Testament that tell us how—and how not—to treat one another. As we obey these directives in our relationships, we reflect to the world the perfect love of Jesus. (Emphasis is added in all cases.)

♥ Love from Your Heart ♥

1 Peter 1:22: Now that you have purified yourselves by obeying the truth so that you have sincere love for each other, love *one another* deeply, from the heart.

♥ Love to Encourage ♥

2 Corinthians 13:11: Finally, brothers and sisters, rejoice! Strive for full restoration, encourage *one another*, be of one mind, live in peace. And the God of love and peace will be with you.

1 Thessalonians 5:11: Therefore encourage *one another* and build each other up, just as in fact you are doing.

Hebrews 3:13: But encourage *one another* daily, as long as it is called "Today," so that none of you may be hardened by sin's deceitfulness.

♥ Love to Show Humility and Impart Honor ♥

Romans 12:10: Be devoted to *one another* in love. Honor *one another* above yourselves.

Ephesians 5:21: Submit to *one another* out of reverence for Christ.

1 Peter 3:8: Finally, all of you, be like-minded, be sympathetic, love *one another*, be compassionate and humble.

1 Peter 5:5: In the same way, you who are younger, submit yourselves to your elders. All of you, clothe yourselves with humility toward *one another*, because, "God opposes the proud but shows favor to the humble."

♥ Love with Your Words ♥

Ephesians 5:19–20: Speaking to *one another* with psalms, hymns, and songs from the Spirit. Sing and make music from your heart to the Lord, always giving thanks to God the Father for everything, in the name of our Lord Jesus Christ.

Colossians 3:16: Let the message of Christ dwell among you richly as you teach and admonish *one another* with all wisdom through psalms, hymns, and songs from the Spirit, singing to God with gratitude in your hearts.

James 4:11: Brothers and sisters, do not slander *one another*. Anyone who speaks against a brother or sister or judges them speaks against the law and judges it. When you judge the law, you are not keeping it, but sitting in judgment on it.

James 5:9: Don't grumble against *one another*, brothers and sisters, or you will be judged. The Judge is standing at the door!

♥ Love by Serving ♥

John 13:14: Now that I, your Lord and Teacher, have washed your feet, you also should wash *one another's* feet.

Galatians 5:13: You, my brothers and sisters, were called to be free. But do not use your freedom to indulge the flesh; rather, serve *one another* humbly in love.

Hebrews 10:24–25: And let us consider how we may spur *one another* on toward love and good deeds, not giving up meeting together, as some are in the habit of doing, but encouraging *one another*—and all the more as you see the Day approaching.

1 Peter 4:9: Offer hospitality to *one another* without grumbling.

♥ Love without Stopping ♥

Romans 13:8: Let no debt remain outstanding, except the continuing debt to love *one another*, for whoever loves others has fulfilled the law.

Hebrews 13:1: Keep on loving *one another* as brothers and sisters.

♥ Love to Demonstrate How God Treats Us ♥

John 13:34–35: A new command I give you: Love *one another*. As I have loved you, so you must love *one another*. By this everyone will know that you are my disciples, if you love *one another*.

Ephesians 4:32: Be kind and compassionate to *one another*, forgiving each other, just as in Christ God forgave you.

Philippians 2:5: In your relationships with *one another*, have the same mindset as Christ Jesus.

1 John 1:7: But if we walk in the light, as he is in the light, we have fellowship with *one another*, and the blood of Jesus, his Son, purifies us from all sin.

1 John 4:7: Dear friends, let us love *one another*, for love comes from God. Everyone who loves has been born of God and knows God.

1 John 4:11: Dear friends, since God so loved us, we also ought to love *one another*.

1 John 4:12: No one has ever seen God; but if we love *one another*, God lives in us and his love is made complete in us.

♥ Love Because God Commands You To ♥

1 John 3:23: And this is his command: to believe in the name of his Son, Jesus Christ, and to love *one another* as he commanded us.

1 Thessalonians 4:9: Now about your love for *one another* we do not need to write to you, for you yourselves have been taught by God to love each other.

1 John 3:11: For this is the message you heard from the beginning: We should love *one another*.

2 John 1:5: And now, dear lady, I am not writing you a new command but one we have had from the beginning. I ask that we love *one another*.

♥ Love to Promote Harmony ♥

Romans 12:16: Live in harmony with *one another*. Do not be proud, but be willing to associate with people of low position. Do not be conceited.

Romans 14:13: Therefore let us stop passing judgment on *one another*. Instead, make up your mind not to put any stumbling block or obstacle in the way of a brother or sister.

Romans 15:7: Accept *one another*, then, just as Christ accepted you, in order to bring praise to God.

1 Corinthians 1:10: I appeal to you, brothers and sisters, in the name of our Lord Jesus Christ, that all of you agree with *one another* in what you say and that there be no divisions among you, but that you be perfectly united in mind and thought.

Ephesians 4:2: Be completely humble and gentle; be patient, bearing with *one another* in love.

Colossians 3:13: Bear with each other and forgive *one another* if any of you has a grievance against someone. Forgive as the Lord forgave you.

♥ Love to Show Holy Affection ♥

Romans 16:16: Greet *one another* with a holy kiss. All the churches of Christ send greetings.

1 Corinthians 16:20: All the brothers and sisters here send you greetings. Greet *one another* with a holy kiss.

2 Corinthians 13:12: Greet *one another* with a holy kiss.

1 Peter 5:14: Greet *one another* with a kiss of love. Peace to all of you who are in Christ. (Okay . . . maybe we will want to make it a "holy high-five" to be safe!)

A HEAVENLY RECIPE
RIGHT HERE ON EARTH

And they sang a new song, saying: "You are worthy to take the scroll and to open its seals, because you were slain, and with your blood you purchased for God persons from every tribe and language and people and nation."

—Revelation 5:9

For all but one year of my life I have lived in small towns within twenty miles of where I was born. These towns, though quaint and friendly, are not what you would call racially or ethnically diverse. Being raised in such an area presents challenges when it comes to getting to know people different from me.

Thankfully, my experience with a friend of my father led me and my whole family to intentionally make efforts to know others who look, live, and worship differently than we do. This friend's name is Ray.

Ray was a coworker of my dad who became very close to our family. He and I have completely different backgrounds and don't share the same race. However, we do share similar hearts. Hearts that love God, family, and ministry. Today, Ray and I are like siblings, and he is even a part of my father's will.

Currently, Brother Ray is the pastor of a church in the big city a few miles south of us. Years ago, when his congregation purchased a larger church building and held their first service there, Ray invited my husband to be one of the guest speakers.

After the service, the church celebrated with a huge home-cooked dinner lovingly made by many of the women of that parish. My family and I were treated like royalty. We were seated at the head table and served the most delicious food, including many dishes I had never tasted before. My children played in the nursery with the other children from the church. We exchanged hugs, well-wishes, and recipes with many from the congregation.

It was an incredible experience, and what made it even more memorable was that we were the only family of our race in attendance that day. And it was good for our children to be in the minority that Sunday.

My first experience of being in the minority was when I went on a college mission trip to a foreign land. The experience was so powerful it changed my perspective on diversity forever. I knew I wanted to encourage my children to intentionally get to know people from all walks of life and various ethnic groups.

As we raised our kids, we have made sure they not only form relationships with those who are different from us, but lovingly serve them as well, just as we were served that day. We have helped put on holiday dinners at a community center that ministers to displaced refugees. When younger, my children saved up some of their allowance money to give to a missionary. And we have sponsored Compassion International children from another continent over the years, helping provide them with food and an education. Getting to know others, and serving them in the process, has made our family's life richer.

The book of Revelation makes it clear that not everyone in heaven will look just like us. There will be people from every tribe and nation and tongue. If heaven will be diverse, we need to make sure we are seeking out diversity while here on earth.

We must seek out new relationships, resist using stereotypes when we speak, and encourage our children (and other young souls in our sphere of influence) to pursue diversity in their friendships. How it warms my heart to see my youngest son, the only one left in high school, snacking with his friends around my kitchen island—friends who, although they share a love of sports, funny videos, and laughter, do not share the same ethnic or racial makeup.

Will you make it a point to purposely reach out to those who look and live differently than you? When you do, you reflect God's heart toward humankind while you also get a little glimpse of heaven. Why, you might just gain some new recipes in the process.

Most of all, the recipe for love.

CHAPTER 3

It's about Time

GIVING OF YOURSELF

Serve God by doing common actions in a heavenly spirit, and then, if your daily calling only leaves you cracks and crevices of time, fill them up with holy service.
—CHARLES SPURGEON

But I trust in you, LORD; I say, "You are my God." My times are in your hands.
—PSALM 31:14–15

It was a sunny April day with powder-blue skies graced with puffy white clouds. I wasn't outside enjoying the gorgeous weather, however. Instead, I sat in a funeral home with the rest of my husband's family, getting ready to receive friends who would offer their condolences.

It was the day of my father-in-law's burial. He'd lived for forty years in the same community, selling cars at the local dealership. He was active in his church and a familiar face around his neighborhood. Naturally, many would show up to offer their sympathies to his widow and the rest of the family who loved him.

Since my husband and I lived several hours away, many of the people who came that day were strangers to us. As I sat greeting them one by one and thanking them for coming, I suddenly heard a familiar voice behind me. Turning, I spotted my good friend Mary standing in the lobby of the funeral home. I could hardly believe my eyes. Although I knew she had been praying for my father-in-law as he battled a terminal illness during his last few months on Earth, I never dreamed she would drive from another state to make an appearance at the visitation. After all, she lived several hours away!

Mary's kind gesture meant more to me than a lovely plant and accompanying sympathy card. Why? Because it cost her something that is very dear to all of us these days: *time.*

In order for Mary to come to the funeral home that day, she had to make sure her three young sons were cared for while she was gone. She had to get dressed for a funeral visitation rather than wear her normal stay-at-home mom outfit of jeans and a T-shirt. She had to put gas in her car and spend over six hours on the road round-trip just to be with me. Stopping her life to use her presence to touch my heart that day cost her time, and I have never forgotten it.

Because Mary's actions had such a great impact on me, it caused me to ponder what a powerful gift our time is. Today we pack our schedules so tightly we barely have any wiggle room. We run from one thing to another to another only to return home again, grab a little sleep, and then get up the next day and do it all over again. Often this leaves us little white space in our schedules for others. Because our day planners are full of activity, our lives are often void of time spent loving other people. So when someone does clear his or her schedule in order to make time for a loving gesture, the impact of the gift is magnified.

Mary's decision to give of her time had a domino effect. It made me determined to attend funerals, even if they are several cities away. Now I too have shocked people because I drove a great distance in order to be with them in a time of grief. Kindness is contagious. Our loving actions might seem like they are only intended for one person. In truth, they are like a cannonball of kindness that splashes waves of love onto the hearts of all nearby.

Have you ever had a friend like Mary, who interrupted her day in order to spend her time doing something kind for you? Think about a time when someone used her time to touch your heart. What happened? Wouldn't it be wonderful to have that same effect on another person today?

On Presenting Presents

I adore holidays. It doesn't matter if it's Christmas, Valentine's Day, Easter, someone's birthday, or even Flag Day. I love to celebrate and celebrate big. Any excuse to throw a party, cook or bake something special, and take a break from the ordinary. And the absolute best part of a celebration? Giving gifts!

Of course no holiday holds more gift-giving than Christmas, and I take the whole gift-giving business pretty seriously. Beginning in the summer, I ask my loved ones for their Christmas wish list, anything from a big-ticket item on down to the trinkets and treats they might fancy in their stocking on Christmas morning. Then I go on a months-long shopping quest. The places and ways to secure Christmas gifts in this day and age are endless. It isn't just department stores where we can purchase presents. There are fancy gourmet shops, high-end boutiques, and thousands of places on the Internet. Most anything we want to find is easily available with the click of a mouse or a touch of the screen. But I have noticed through the years that of all the presents my kids might receive, the ones that matter the most are those that cost time.

Years ago presents took time. While a mother or father might have been able to purchase a store-bought toy, more often than not they made their gifts. Knitting scarves or crafting a piece of furniture kept family members working busily—and often secretly—for many months before Christmas.

Preparing food for Christmas was also a labor of love and a taker of time. Beloved author Laura Ingalls Wilder noted Ma's Christmas preparations in *Little House on the Prairie*: "Ma was busy all day long, cooking good things for Christmas. She baked salt-rising bread and rye 'n' Injun bread, and Swedish crackers, and a huge pan of baked beans, with salt pork and molasses. She baked vinegar pies and dried apple pies, and filled a big jar with cookies."[1] Prairie women didn't just put in an order at the local deli for their Christmas culinary delights. They spent oodles and oodles of time making their food from scratch.

Today we have many shortcuts to celebrations. We can order gifts online and pick up premade dinners at the grocery store. And these can be wonderful tools! But there is something so heartwarming about old-fashioned handmade holiday gifts, decorations, and foods. Making such items from scratch forces us to slow down, spending time with others as we string popcorn or decorate cookies. Spending your time making someone a one-of-a-kind gift is a wonderful way to love that person.

Over the years my kids have received some great Christmas gifts. After having it on their wish list for years, my boys received their own gaming system so they could play sports video games. Much to her delight, after many years of wanting one, my then-teenaged daughter received her first camera. But when the kids—now all teens and young adults—reminisce about their favorites presents, what they mention most are the old-fashioned, made-from-scratch fare. Gifts like the homemade, laminated bookmark I made for our eleven-year-old son. On it I listed all of the phone numbers to the many businesses he tended to call. The sporting goods store. The pet section at the local department store. The archery shop. The hardware store in our small downtown. He could keep this handy reference in his school book for those times when he took a break from his homework to call and ask about the latest bow and arrow model or when the new style of baseball cleats was going to be out. My daughter adored the journal I gave her one year for Christmas. In it I wrote a question for her to answer about her current interests in life. Then it was her turn to write a question to me inquiring about my own middle school years. Back and forth the journal went as we each wrote our thoughts to each other and answered each other's questions. It was a very simple gift. All it took was some time.

Handmade and heartfelt. Such gifts are rare in our hurried and harried culture. Gifts that took time to create or time to give stand out in a unique way. Whether at the holidays or on "ordinary" days, we can be on the lookout for ways to give the gift of time to others.

Delighted to Share

The apostle Paul wrote the books of First and Second Thessalonians to believers in the city of Thessalonica in or around AD 52. Although parts of the books deal with doctrine and theology, their main purpose is simply encouragement. Paul wanted to strengthen the faith of the believers, showing them how to live godly lives in the midst of a worldly culture.

In these letters, Paul recounted the last time he was with this group of Christian brothers and sisters. He remembered the way he preached the gospel to them and his motives for doing so, which were fueled only by love.

He recalled his aim to be gentle among them, revealing his true heart. In the midst of this encouraging letter we read these words: "Just as a nursing mother cares for her children, so we cared for you. Because we loved you so much, we were delighted to share with you not only the gospel of God but our lives as well" (1 Thessalonians 2:7–8).

Paul didn't just speak words; he shared his life. And he did it in a way that was reminiscent of a nursing mother caring lovingly for her children.

As many of you have experienced, being a nursing mother takes a lot out of you both physically and emotionally. You cannot be on your own schedule. You have to interrupt what you are doing in order to nourish the body of your child. To nurse a child you must stop. Sit down. Take time. You must for the moment put your child's needs before your own. Certainly the act of nursing a baby is sharing life in a sacrificial way. This is what Paul did with the young believers in ancient Greece as he and his companions shared their very lives with the members of this newly formed church.

Think about your own life for a moment. Is there someone you recall who "delighted to share" her very life with you? I can think of a few in my own life.

When I became a mother, I didn't have a clue what I was doing. Although I had read all of the latest and greatest how-to-take-care-of-a-baby books, I still had so many questions. Thankfully, I knew a group of mothers in my tiny Midwestern town who were a little farther ahead in the mothering gig than I was, all of them having a couple—or a half dozen—kiddos. The friendship circle of Marcia, Debi, Suzy, and Andie showed me how to mother my own kids. They truly did delight to share their very lives with me.

If I was having trouble with a minor medical issue with my newborn, I could pick up the phone and call one of these women. They knew all about diaper rash. About the best way to trim a baby's fingernails without also clipping her tender skin. (Been there. Snipped that. Ouch!) They knew about eye infections and infant acne. They patiently and lovingly answered my questions about how I could best care for my child's physical needs.

As my children grew older, these women also shared with me concepts for training and disciplining a child—those that worked and those that didn't. Other times they just listened to me either on the phone or in person as I poured out my heart to them. Perhaps I was in a rough place in my marriage. Perhaps I was having trouble with the in-laws. Or maybe I was overwhelmed with the great task of raising another person from infancy to adulthood, teaching a child everything from how to tie shoes to how to drive a car.

These women truly did come alongside me in life's journey. They took time. They gave advice. They didn't brush me aside. Although they couldn't always drop what they were doing to talk to me, they faithfully made a point to reconnect later. They didn't keep their mothering secrets to themselves in a prideful way but were more than happy to guide and direct me, enabling me to see some parenting success. Because they chose to share their lives with me, my life was easier. Sharing life lightens the load and multiplies the blessings as well.

In another book of the New Testament, Paul writes these words: "Carry each other's burdens, and in this way you will fulfill the law of Christ" (Galatians 6:2).

Paul instructs us to help to lighten the load of others, because when we encourage, cheer, help, guide, or simply do life with another person, we let them see a little snippet of Christ and his love. Our acts don't have to be complicated or grand. Even simple acts of service and offerings of time can have a monumental effect in the life of another.

Sharing Life 101

What are some ways we can share our very lives with other people? I'm so glad you asked. Try any of the following suggestions. You're sure to bring a smile not only to the recipient's face but to yours as well. Those who make a point to bring joy into the life of another cannot help but experience it themselves.

HELP SOMEONE CHECK SOMETHING OFF THEIR TO-DO LIST THIS WEEKEND.

Is the weekend coming up? We typically have more downtime on the weekends. Maybe you could get up a little earlier than normal this Saturday in order to help someone accomplish that looming task on their to-do list. Does your mother-in-law need her garage swept out and straightened? Could the elderly neighbor use help filling out his insurance forms? How about that single mom at church who mentioned that she needs to shop for a new stove? Brainstorm how you might help someone else whittle away at their to-do list by giving a little time this weekend.

LIGHTEN A DOMESTIC LOAD.

Just living life can be exhausting, especially if you have a home to keep up or children to care for. Think of someone in your life who might be overwhelmed on the home front. What is something you could do to help lighten the load? Could you show up with a few laundry baskets and kidnap their dirty laundry? Take it home. Wash it. Dry it. Fold it all neatly. Then show up again with the chore done and a plate of treats for them to enjoy while they put their feet up for a few minutes.

Maybe you could grant the gift of a housecleaning session. Kick your friend out of her house for an hour or two. Show up with a bucket full of cleaning supplies and give her home a thorough scrubbing. Clean mirrors and counters. Vacuum and sweep her floors. Mop and dust. Then leave a little basket with some treats and trinkets chosen just for her. Doing this will not only relieve her of an often unpleasant chore, it will help her clear her mind and get out of the house for a bit.

What other domestic duties could you do for a friend, family member, or neighbor? If you have older kids, is it something they could participate in as well? Sometimes just a few hours on your part can make a huge impact on someone else's life.

SPEND A LITTLE OF YOUR TIME HELPING
SOMEONE ELSE SAVE SOME OF THEIRS.

Is there an errand you need to run today? Do you need to go to the dry cleaners, the grocery store, or the drugstore? Let your outing save someone else some time. Call your friend to see if she has anything that needs to be picked up from the dry cleaners. See if that busy mom down the street whose husband works long hours needs something from the grocery store. Instead of her having to tote her children along for the outing, she can stay at home while you grab a few groceries for her. Is there someone you know who is at home recovering from a recent surgery? See if she needs anything from the drugstore. You can use your common, weekly outings to show love to someone else.

THINK IN MULTIPLES OF TWO.

When I was first married, an older woman from church and I were discussing nightly dinner preparation. She told me, "Cook once. Eat twice." I wasn't sure what she meant, so I asked her to explain. She said whenever I cooked a meal, I should make a habit to double the recipe. That way I'd only cook once, but my family would enjoy two meals for the effort. So, for example, if you are making a pan of lasagna and you know it freezes well, make two pans of lasagna. Wrap one tightly in foil and pop it in the freezer. Then pull it out on a busy day and have a main dish ready without time or mess. I took her advice and have done this for years, not only with lasagna, but also with homemade pot pies, meatloaf, spaghetti sauce, barbecued meatballs, and my famous broccoli Swiss quiche.

This little trick can also be a way to help out someone else. Do you know a woman who recently gave birth or adopted a child? Is someone dealing with a death in the family? Is someone in the process of moving who is up to her eyeballs in boxes? Is a family at church busy preparing for a wedding, leaving little time to cook? Give away your extra freezer meal.

Scout around for recipes of delicious meals that freeze and reheat well. Then do what my church friend told me—cook once, eat twice! It really isn't much more difficult to assemble a second meal. By spending just a little extra time making a double batch of one thing—even cookies or muffins—you will be blessing another family or individual with some yummy food and saving them time as well.

What if you're not a cook or work full time and simply don't have the wherewithal to create a home-cooked meal? A rotisserie chicken, some deli coleslaw and baked beans, and a side of rolls makes a homey, nourishing meal. One of my friends works full time and when she delivered this grocery-bought meal after I had a baby, she was apologetic that it wasn't homemade. But I treasured the gift of sacrificial time and thoughtfulness that had gone into the meal and enjoyed it just as much as the home-cooked ones I received.

SPEAK THE POWERFUL WORDS "ME TOO."

Sharing life with someone doesn't mean just helping to meet their physical needs or assisting with tasks around the house. Sometimes sharing life means letting another person know that you understand what she is going through. As author and theologian C. S. Lewis beautifully stated, "Friendship is born at that moment when one person says to another: 'What! You too? I thought I was the only one.'"

When Todd and I had been married about three years, we became pregnant for the first time. I was ecstatic and could not wait to welcome our sweet baby the following summer. Just a few months into my pregnancy, however, things began to go wrong. After a few concerning trips to the doctor and an ultrasound, we discovered our baby's heart was no longer beating. I was sent home to wait for the baby to deliver on its own. Those several days were some of the darkest of my life.

Our friends and church family were wonderful. People brought over meals. Some sent flowers. A few sent a card or handwritten note letting me know how sorry they were that our baby's life had ended in miscarriage. But the person who most ministered to my soul, and showed me love in a tangible way, was my friend Debi.

Debi didn't show up at my house with a casserole or a bouquet of daisies, though that would have been very thoughtful. She showed up with heartfelt empathy from an experience in her own past. She knocked on my door one evening and when I opened it, she was standing there with Godiva dark chocolate and a box of tissues. As we sat together on the sofa in our tiny living room, she told me about her own miscarriage years before. She recalled how much it helped her and her husband to actually give the baby a name so that in the future they wouldn't just refer to him as "the baby we lost." (They had named their baby Jesse. We named ours Kelly.) She also recalled her feelings at the time. She talked about what others did that was helpful. And about some things people had said that, although well intentioned, were painful. We cried and ate dark chocolate. Her words and her presence that evening were a tangible display of two of the most powerful words we can say to someone going through a tumultuous or sorrowful time: "Me too."

"Me too" lets us know that someone understands our pain. It softens the blow as we realize we are not the only ones who have ever dealt with this issue or suffered the same tragedy. Is there someone in your life today who needs you to show up—tissues and dark chocolate in hand—to speak the powerful phrase, "Me too"?

LISTEN FOR THOSE HEART DROPS AND RESPOND.

As I mentioned in the first chapter, we need to live alert, listening for heart drops, those "read between the lines" gut-level feelings we have about someone's needs based on really trying to listen to their heart.

Did you sense a coworker was discouraged this week? Did you have the feeling when you hung up the phone the other night that your cousin was feeling defeated? Did a brief conversation in the grocery store with the parent of one of your child's friends give you the impression that their marriage might be in trouble? All of these inklings are heart drops. They speak to our soul, whispering to us that someone is in need of encouragement and a gift of timely attention.

Take inventory of recent conversations with those in your life, whether close friends and family members or perhaps just an acquaintance or coworker. Has someone been giving you heart drops? If so, who? Now prayerfully consider how you might encourage that person. Could you phone them? Text them a Bible verse? Write them a note and drop it in the mail? People need to know that others care. Let's not become so busy that we turn a deaf ear to the heart drops around us. Who might the Lord be calling you to encourage today?

Nine Doors Down

Sharing my ideas and stories about loving others is a joy. But sometimes I have blown it. Or I simply was not living alert and missed an opportunity. The crisp fall air on my backyard deck today reminds me of one such incident. It happened five years ago in September and affected me profoundly.

Back then, we had been living in our new neighborhood for about two years. During that time I had seen this woman on my walks. Sometimes she was rolling her trash can out to the curb. Or in her front yard watering her flowers. I'd smile and say hi, and then I'd pop my headphones back in and keep walking to my house, just nine doors down. After all, my neighborhood is big; my life is busy.

Then one day, there were flashing lights, sirens, and all things alarming in our neighborhood. *A fire, maybe?* I thought as I returned from an errand-running venture. My mama's heart raced. My twelve-year-old son was home alone. Had he burnt some toast and set the smoke alarm system blaring? Or worse?

As my car approached, I saw it was not my house, but another house nine doors down. Relief for my soul.

And though the rescue vehicles were parked in front of my nine-doors-down neighbor's house, no fire appeared to blaze there either. "Must have been a false alarm," I reasoned to myself.

Two days later, I heard the awful news. No fire. No smoke. Just a terribly saddened soul.

You see, just nine doors down, something happened in the mind of my nameless, flower-watering, smile-and-say-hello fellow human being. Something told her this life wasn't worth living anymore. And she agreed.

Now her heart no longer beats. Her flowers still grow, but she can't water them anymore. I can still walk by her house, lost deeply in the Jesus-music blaring on my iPod. Staring straight ahead. Rushing to the next thing on my to-do list for the day.

Nine doors down, there will be no more hand-waves. No smiles as I stroll by. And no more thoughts of *I should stop and find out her name*. I hadn't really met this gal yet. If I'd reached out and befriended her, would she have seen Jesus in our friendship?

Could we have walked the neighborhood streets together? Maybe gone for coffee to get to know each other a bit? Would a glimpse of the perfect God in the life of an imperfect me perhaps have beckoned her to have a relationship with him too? Would she have found

God's purpose and peace instead of looking for a way to end her emotional pain?

God only knows.

I am a woman who wants to love God, but so often I am too busy to love the people he puts in my path. Such love is important, more important than all the sacrifices we could make. "'Love your neighbor as yourself.' There is no commandment greater than these," Jesus said (Mark 12:31).

Although this situation saddens me terribly, I cannot beat myself up about it. But I can do something. So can you. We can pause, permitting God to tap us on the heart, gently interrupt us, and rearrange our day.

We can purpose to go deeper—beyond a hurried "Hi!" to an authentic "How are you?"

When God knocks on our hearts, we can knock on their doors.

Will you do it? Will you try? Then once you've reached out, leave the results to God. Our job is obedience. God will do the rest.

Trust me, it is awful to get to know your neighbor through the tales and tears of her relatives at a memorial service. I wish I had made the time and gotten to know her personally.

May we all respond to those taps on our hearts today and not ignore them. God just may use us as he saves a life.

After all, remember it isn't that far of a walk . . .

It's just nine doors down.

Father, may I not be content to keep your love to myself. May I make it my aim, like Paul, to share my very life with others. It may be family members. It may be a friend. Or it may be a neighbor I barely know. Make my heart sensitive. Let me hear your gentle whispers as they prompt me to reach out and give of my time and resources. I want to live and love like your Son. In his holy name I pray. Amen.

Five Fab Freezer Meals

Here are five of my go-to meals to make for someone in need. The recipient can pop them in the oven the day you deliver them or stash them away in the freezer for a crazy-busy or stressful day yet to come. Each recipe makes two main dishes—one to give away and one to keep for your family.

Cheesy Chicken Enchilada Casserole

INGREDIENTS FOR 2 CASSEROLES:

6 c. shredded cooked chicken
1 medium onion, finely chopped
2 t. minced garlic
2 (4 oz.) cans diced green chili peppers
2 (10 oz.) cans diced tomatoes with green chili peppers
2 (16 oz.) jars taco sauce
2 packages taco seasoning
2 (16 oz.) cans refried beans
16 (8-inch) soft flour tortillas
32 oz. sharp shredded cheddar cheese

DIRECTIONS:

Preheat oven to 350 degrees.

In a large bowl, mix the chicken, onion, garlic, chili peppers, tomatoes, taco sauce, and taco seasoning.

Coat two 9-inch round casserole dishes with cooking spray. Spread a thin layer of the chicken mixture on the bottom of both pans.

Spread a thin layer of refried beans on a tortilla, making sure to go all the way to the edges, and place it in the dish on top of the chicken mixture with the beans face-up. Top it with another flour tortilla, followed by more meat mixture, then a layer of cheese. Repeat the pattern of tortilla with beans, plain tortilla, meat, and cheese until all the tortillas are used (about 8 tortillas per 9-inch casserole dish), ending with a top layer of meat mixture and cheese all the way to the edges.

Bake uncovered for 20 to 30 minutes in the preheated oven, or until cheese is slightly brown and bubbly.

For freezing: Wrap pans tightly with foil and freeze them. When ready to use, bake uncovered at 350 degrees for about 35–45 minutes until cheese is bubbly and dish is thoroughly heated. ♥

Creamy Tetrazzini

INGREDIENTS FOR 2 PANS:

1 (12 oz.) package spaghetti pasta

1 (14.5 oz.) can chicken broth

4 c. chopped cooked chicken or turkey

3 c. chopped ham

2 (10.5 oz.) cans cream of chicken soup

2 c. sour cream

8 oz. fresh sliced mushrooms

1/4 c. (1/2 stick) butter

2 T. olive oil

3 c. grated sharp cheddar cheese

3/4 c. grated Parmesan cheese (fresh is best)

1/8 t. ground pepper

1 t. salt

DIRECTIONS:

Sauté mushrooms in olive oil and butter until tender. Season with salt and pepper. In a separate pot, cook pasta 6–8 minutes, until al dente. Drain and rinse with cold water.

In a large bowl, mix soup and sour cream. Stir in can of chicken broth. Add in mushrooms and blend well. Add meats, pasta, and cheddar cheese. Stir until well combined.

Spray two 9 x 13 inch pans with cooking spray and spread in tetrazzini. Sprinkle Parmesan on top of casserole. Cover with foil.

Bake at 350 degrees for 40–50 minutes or until heated through.

For freezing: Wrap tightly in foil and freeze. The day before cooking, place tetrazzini in the fridge to thaw. Bake, covered, 45–60 minutes at 350 degrees or until thoroughly heated. If tetrazzini is still partially frozen before baking, allow more cooking time. You may also freeze the tetrazzini in a two-gallon freezer bag and pour it into a pan on baking day. ♥

Broccoli, Ham, and Swiss Quiche

INGREDIENTS FOR 2 PIE PANS:

10 eggs, lightly beaten
1 c. whole milk
1 c. half and half
1 1/2 c. frozen broccoli flowerets, diced
1 c. diced ham

3 c. Swiss cheese, shredded
1/2 c. green onions, chopped
1/2 t. salt
1/4 t. pepper
2 (9-inch) refrigerated piecrusts

DIRECTIONS:

To bake immediately, mix all ingredients but the crust in a large bowl. Roll crust in a 9-inch pie pan. Pour mixture into crust. Bake at 350 degrees for 50–60 minutes, or until a knife comes out clean. Allow quiche to sit for 10–15 minutes before cutting.

For freezing: Mix all ingredients but the crust in a bowl and then pour them into a gallon zip-top bag. Remove excess air, seal, and place within another zip-top bag to prevent freezer burn. Place in freezer.

Print cooking instructions and place it between the bag with the egg mixture and the outer bag. Store flat to speed up defrosting. Make sure to freeze the piecrust too.

Instructions for cooking from frozen: Thaw quiche bag and piecrust in refrigerator for approximately 24–36 hours. Roll crust in a pie pan. Pour mixture into crust.

Preheat oven to 350 degrees. Bake uncovered for approximately 60–70 minutes or until an inserted knife comes out clean. The top should be lightly brown. Allow quiche to sit for 10–15 minutes before cutting. ♥

Potato-and-Cheese-Stuffed Barbecue Meatloaf

INGREDIENTS FOR 2 MEATLOAVES:

5 lbs. lean ground beef
6 slices white bread, torn into small pieces
4 eggs, lightly beaten
1/2 c. Dijon mustard
2 t. salt
1/4 t. black pepper
1 c. finely minced onion
4 c. (16 oz.) shredded sharp cheddar cheese
3 c. frozen shredded hash brown potatoes
3 c. barbecue sauce, divided (Sweet Baby Ray's brand is our favorite!)

DIRECTIONS:

Mix beef, bread, eggs, mustard, salt, pepper, and onion with one cup of barbecue sauce. Pat mixture out on a large piece of wax paper to form two 10 x 12 inch rectangles. Sprinkle half the potatoes and half the cheese over each section of meat. Roll up jelly roll–style starting at the short end and lifting paper off of the counter as you go to help the meat to form into a roll. Seal seam well, lift the roll up off of the wax paper, and place seam side down in a 9 x 13 inch pan that has been sprayed with cooking spray. Pour remaining barbecue sauce evenly over the top of both meat rolls.

If serving immediately, bake at 350 degrees for one hour, making sure no more pink remains in the center. Baste with additional sauce, if desired.

For freezing: Follow directions above except do not cover with additional sauce. Place meat roll on a large piece of plastic wrap and roll up, securing tightly. Wrap again in a layer of foil. Freeze. Thaw in the fridge for 24 hours before baking. Remove from foil and plastic wrap and place in a 9 x 13 inch pan that has been sprayed with cooking spray. Cover with additional barbecue sauce. Bake, uncovered, at 350 degrees for an hour, making sure no more pink remains in the center. Baste with additional sauce, if desired. ♥

Italian Stuffed Shells

INGREDIENTS FOR 2 PANS:

2 (12 oz.) boxes jumbo pasta shells
32 oz. small curd cottage cheese
32 oz. ricotta cheese
4 c. shredded Italian blend or mozzarella cheese
1 1/2 c. grated Parmesan cheese
6 eggs, lightly beaten
1 t. oregano
2 t. basil
1 1/2 t. salt
1 t. black pepper
2 jars (28 oz. each) spaghetti sauce

DIRECTIONS:

Cook shells according to box directions but for only half the recommended time. Drain and rinse with cold water.

In a large mixing bowl, place all other ingredients except the spaghetti sauce, and stir until well blended.

Using a large spoon, stuff shells with cheese mixture and place on wax-paper-lined baking sheets.

To make immediately, spoon 1/2 cup of sauce into the bottom of each of two 9 x 13 inch baking dishes that have been sprayed with cooking spray. Place the shells on top of the sauce. (Or just make one pan and then freeze remaining shells per instructions below.) Cover well with remaining sauce and seal pan with foil. Bake at 350 degrees for 45–55 minutes or until shells are heated through and sauce is bubbly.

For freezing: Once all shells are stuffed and placed on wax-paper-lined cookie sheets, place sheet in freezer for about an hour. Remove shells and split them evenly between two zip-top gallon freezer bags and return to freezer for longer-term storage. Make sure to remove excess air before sealing bags.

When ready to bake, spoon half a jar of sauce into bottom of a 9 x 13 inch baking dish that has been sprayed with cooking spray. Top with one bag of shells. Spoon rest of sauce over the top of shells. Cover dish with foil, seal tightly, and bake at 350 degrees for 55–65 minutes or until shells are heated through and sauce is bubbly. ♥

CHAPTER 4

Who Makes Your Day

NOTICING THE NECESSARY PEOPLE

The noblest art is that of making others happy.
—PHINEAS TAYLOR BARNUM

Therefore, as God's chosen people, holy and dearly loved, clothe yourselves with compassion, kindness, humility, gentleness and patience.
—COLOSSIANS 3:12

My two small children huddled together, giggling with glee. It was a special day that my kids had looked forward to for weeks. It wasn't Christmas or Easter. Not even the Fourth of July, when they scored candy at the local parade. Nope. It was Mr. Brown Day.

Let me explain.

My husband and I had been talking with our kids about not only *saying* we love others but *doing* something to show it. One day during family devotions we asked Mitchell and Kenna if there was anyone they would like to show love to in a creative and tangible way. We encouraged them to think of a "necessary person" we knew who helped us to get life done each week. It didn't take them long to both come up with the same person—Mr. Brown!

Mr. Brown was our mailman. But he wasn't your average, run-of-the-mill postal worker. Mr. Brown delivered more than just the commonplace letters, bills, and packages each day. He delivered smiles and encouragement to those along his route. He didn't see each house on his course as merely a destination to drop letters. He saw the people who lived inside the brick-and-mortar homes. Never too busy to chat for a few minutes with a lonely widow, or to ask a youngster about his upcoming Little League game, Mr. Brown got to know the folks along his route. Our kids couldn't wait to surprise him one afternoon when he brought us our daily mail.

In order to prepare for Mr. Brown Day, we took our children to the local dollar store and told them to let their imaginations run wild dreaming up gifts for Mr. Brown's goody bag. So they purchased a squirt gun for him to use to ward off the neighborhood dogs. They grabbed a few candy bars (truthfully, their favorites, not necessarily his!). They bought a few other trinkets and then asked if we could purchase a gift certificate to a local restaurant so he could take Mrs. Brown out for a "fancy dinner."

Apparently they felt our neighborhood Dairy Queen served a good supper, and so we stopped there to snag a gift card for him and the Missus. We baked cookies and made some fresh-squeezed lemonade. We also purchased some party blowers and confetti to use on the big day. Then, when the day came—a random Tuesday—we hid inside our front door and waited.

Just like clockwork, he rounded the corner that sunny spring afternoon. (Well, maybe not like clockwork. Mr. Brown's uncanny ability to converse with the people along his route did have a downside. Sometimes he got behind schedule from all the chitchat!) My preschool son, Mitchell, was our lookout scout. When he saw Mr. Brown coming down our maple-lined street, he whispered excitedly, "Here he comes!"

We continued to crouch down underneath our picture window. Our old wooden door was open and just our screen door stood between us and our favorite mailman. Just as he stepped up on the porch, we flung open the door, blew our party honkers, and tossed confetti in the air.

"Surprise!" we shouted. "It's Mr. Brown, best mailman in town! Today is officially Mr. Brown Day!"

To say he was surprised would be a gross understatement. He immediately wanted to know what all the ruckus was about. I sat and watched as my sweet children explained to him what they had in their treat basket for him. He chuckled at the squirt gun they'd chosen. He raved about the gift certificate to Dairy Queen and assured them that Mrs. Brown would think that was a luxurious treat and would wear her fanciest dress to the outing. He snacked on a cookie and sipped the lemonade. And then, the moment came. He asked them what in the world ever prompted them to create this new holiday just for him.

My daughter Kenna, a kindergartner that year, told him we had been studying in the Bible about not just saying we love people but really showing them. And she and Mitchell had chosen him!

Mr. Brown smiled, gave each child a hug, and patted baby Spencer's head. Then he went on his way but with an added spring in his step. I didn't really think much more about our front porch shower of love until about a week later.

I was out front, once again trying to clean off all the little fingerprints on our living room picture window, when I heard the familiar sound of Mr. Brown's feet coming up my front walkway. I turned around and greeted him. His response made my heart swell with joy.

It was a sunny day and he was wearing sunglasses. He slowly removed them, shook his head from side to side, and declared, "I have to tell you. I'm still not over Mr. Brown Day." And then he said something I could not believe. His voice cracking, he continued, "You know, I have been a mailman on this route, delivering mail on this exact street, for thirty-three years, and no one has *ever* done anything like what your family did for me. Sure, people remember me at Christmas. But no one has ever reached out to me on a random Tuesday afternoon to say that they appreciate what I do." Visibly choked up, he concluded, "Thank you for Mr. Brown Day."

Wow! Thirty-three years of faithful service and no one ever thought to thank him other than at Christmas time. Now don't go thinking our family is all amazing. It took us almost eight years of his being our mail carrier to think of the idea! But it just goes to show you that there are necessary people all around us whose lives might be deeply touched by a random, out-of-the-ordinary act of true kindness.

Looking at Them but Seeing Him

Noticing the necessary people in our life isn't just a hobby. It isn't just something we engage in so we can snap a picture, upload it on social media, and have everyone elect us humanitarian of the year. We don't do it to boast. Or to get a blessing in return. We show love to the necessary people in our lives because when we do, we are acknowledging the fact that all humans are created in the image of God. As the very beginning of the Bible states: "So God created human beings in his own image. In the image of God he created them; male and female he created them" (Genesis 1:27 NLT).

Every day and every week, our lives naturally inter-sect with many people, all of whom bear the image of God. When we look beyond ourselves—and beyond the flaws and quirks of others—we see God. We have an opportunity not only to greet these necessary people face-to-face but to witness God's very image in them.

Each person in his or her role demonstrates some aspect of God's character and his care for us. Our hair-stylist "notes every hair on our head" (Matthew 10:30;

Luke 12:7)! Our lawn service creates a beautiful natural setting for us to enjoy (Genesis 9:3). Our butcher provides delicious food to nourish our family (Proverbs 31:15). Our carpet cleaner makes our carpet "as white as snow" (Isaiah 1:18; Psalm 51:7)! (Well, except for that one pesky grape juice stain!) Our doctor—and other medical professionals—help us to live, and breathe, and have our being (Acts 17:28). Yes, everywhere we look we see reflections of God's creative genius and loving care in the people who serve us.

Our lives can have more meaning and seem more of an exciting adventure if we stop to notice these necessary people. As we recognize them as image bearers of God himself, we will be more cognizant not only to thank them for their service but to do something to encourage them as well.

Noticing Those Necessary People

Who are the necessary people in your life? Many of them help you week in and week out. Let's draw them out of the background and bring them to the forefront in our thinking. Survey your life for a moment. Who helps you get things done? Think through the following list. Perhaps you will want to even circle any of them that apply to your life.

When I think of my life, these are the necessary people that come to mind:

- ♥ The mail carrier (It's no longer Mr. Brown but a new mail lady.)
- ♥ The garbage collectors

♥ Our doctor, dentist, dental hygienist, and optometrist

♥ My son's teachers, principal, coaches, school secretary, lunchroom workers, and athletic director

♥ Our pastor and church staff

♥ The grocery store clerk and bagger

♥ My hairstylist

♥ The local police officers, firefighters, and other first responders

♥ The barista at my favorite coffee shop

♥ My boss and coworkers

♥ Servicemen and women in the armed forces

I'm sure you can think of many more!

All of these people are necessary. They help me—and my family—to get life done. Consider some of the following ways that you might reach out to show them that you care and that you are grateful for the service they provide for you faithfully year after year.

TAKE INVENTORY AND CHOOSE JUST ONE PERSON.

Using the list above, craft your own catalog of the necessary people in your life. But don't let this exercise overwhelm you. You don't have to do something for everyone on your list. Just pray about one person to begin with. If you have a husband or children or other family members living with you, gather their ideas and opinions as well. Then select one person—much like our family did with Mr. Brown—to be the recipient of your love.

BE NOSY AND EAVESDROP.

The next couple of times you are around your chosen necessary person, be a bit inquisitive. Ask questions. Take notice of the things they enjoy or their hobbies. Do they have a favorite candy bar? How about a soft drink you notice them chugging often? Is there a professional sports team or television show they follow? Ask a few leading questions and also just be observant. This very well will provide you some ideas of what to do to show them love.

BRAINSTORM AND BUY.

Once you have come up with a few ideas of their interests, brainstorm what you might do. Will you put together a surprise day like we did for Mr. Brown? Will you send them on a fun outing that includes their favorite sports team or musical group? Will you anonymously leave them a basket full of goodies along with a handwritten note? Begin to craft your plan and purchase the needed items.

DETONATE A LOVE BOMB.

It is a total blast (pun intended!) to catch your necessary person in the middle of doing what it is that they do best and detonate your "love bomb." Take along your gift to your doctor or dentist appointment. Interrupt your favorite barista in the middle of the day. Set your gift basket on top of your garbage container for the garbage collector. Drop by the school to thank your child's teacher or school administrative assistant. It will mean so much that you remembered them with this gift of love on a totally random and ordinary day.

SEND A CARE PACKAGE.

You can always use the postal service or another shipping company to deliver your love. This works especially well if you want to remain anonymous. And if you know a service man or service woman who is serving overseas, show your gratitude and appreciation for them by sending them a package of love. Be sure to check websites for all of the particulars about mailing a package to a member of the armed services.

GIVE THE GIFT OF WORDS.

One of the most heartfelt gifts you can give someone is the gift of your words. While writing letters used to be very common, today it's seldom practiced. So grab a notecard or some stationery and a pen to express your thoughts. It helps to be specific. Rather than merely jotting down, "Thank you for all that you do," mention a particular incident. For example, you might write to the Little League coach, "I saw how you took the extra time to teach my son the proper way to slide into home plate after he failed to do it right and it cost our team a run. It meant so much to me that you didn't yell at him for doing wrong but instead patiently showed him how to do it right next time. The world needs more caring and conscientious coaches like you!"

CREATE A DOMINO EFFECT.

Give a gift that keeps on giving. Purchase a platter, either brand-new from a department store or vintage from a resale shop or secondhand store. Whip up some homemade granola bars or cookies or muffins. Deliver it to one of your necessary people, and attach a note that states that once they have enjoyed their goody, they are to choose a person in their life and repeat the deed. I knew one such person who tried this idea, and about two years after she started the dominoes falling, the plate showed up back at her house! Maybe it's true that what goes around comes around.

DON'T FORGET TO RECRUIT THE FAMILY TO HELP!

Never underestimate the ability of family members, no matter how small or how old, to contribute to the mission of blessing others. Ask your small children for their ideas. Include grandma or grandpa. Make it a family affair. Our kids have shared such ideas as giving a twenty dollar bill and a hearty thanks to the mentally challenged teen who corrals the grocery carts in the store's parking lot and baking cookies for the elderly man who sells his vegetables at our town's farmers market. Including everyone adds a special touch of beauty as you get to view through their eyes who they find necessary in their life. You may even want to take turns letting a different person from the family choose someone to bless each month.

AND MOST IMPORTANTLY—PRAY!

Don't just show love tangibly and outwardly to the people in your life but also remember them in prayer—both before you show them love and afterward. The most important gift you could ever give anyone is the gift of prayer. It not only helps them, it enables you to connect your heart to theirs when you petition God on their behalf, asking his greatest blessings over their life. Including the necessary people in your life on your prayer list will also help to grow your gratitude for them. So jot their names on your prayer list and leave them there!

——— R-E-S-P-E-C-T ———

It truly is a fun and memory-making endeavor to take time to show love to a necessary person in your life. But there is another way we can show ongoing love to these people. That is by showing something that is often forgotten in our society: good old-fashioned respect. The Bible tells us, "Respect everyone, and love the family of believers. Fear God, and respect the king" (1 Peter 2:17 NLT).

Both my husband and I were taught from an early age to respect those around us, especially how we talk to them. We have tried to pass this lesson on to our own children, but I wasn't sure if they were getting it. Then one rainy afternoon I got a peek into one of our children's lives at the local middle school.

Our youngest son, an eighth grader at the time,

and I were walking down the school hallway follow-ing a meeting with the vice principal. As I opened my umbrella to ward off the chilly shower outside, I heard a woman's voice pipe up, "Hello? Excuse me. May I ask you a question?"

I turned to see one of the lunchroom workers walk-ing toward me.

"Are you Spencer's mother?" she inquired.

"Yes," I answered. "Is there something wrong?" My heart fretted. I had just left the vice principal's office where my son sat busted for pulling a stunt which he and his buddies found completely hilarious, but which the substitute teacher saw no humor in. I was not bursting with parental pride. Now I feared he'd also misbehaved in the lunchroom.

"Oh, no. Nothing is wrong at all!" she declared. "I just wanted to tell you how respectful your son is. He never fails to flash a huge smile and thank me when I hand him his food, or ask if I am having a good day. And he addresses me as 'ma'am' and calls the custodian 'sir.' Such a fine and respectful son you've raised!"

To say her words thrilled this mama's heart would be an understatement. In fact, it was a little kiss from God that day when this thoughtful school employee pointed out a positive quality she saw in my teenage son's behavior.

Respect is a rare commodity these days. In person—and especially online—snark and sarcasm often rule. Talking down to someone or insulting one another is the new norm. For adults and for kids, respect is often nowhere to be found.

No longer does society at large use terms like *sir* and *ma'am* when speaking to a stranger. Addressing elders with terms of esteem is rare as well. And having respect for authority seems to have gone out of style long ago.

First Peter 2:17 refers not just to respecting those in authority, such as a police officer, a judge, or the president. It goes so far as to say that we are to respect everyone.

Everyone.

Applying that biblical truth to our necessary people, does this mean respecting the young man who cleans your carpet, greeting him cheerfully, and thanking him for his work when he finishes? Yes, of course.

What about the difficult teacher, the one who seems to target your child? Yep. Her too.

How about the contractor that you've caught cutting corners and cheating? Or the painter who shows every indication of having a full-blown and inappropriate infatuation with you? Yes, even they need your respect, even as you gently but firmly push back on their poor behavior. (More about showing love and respect to such difficult people coming up in chapter eight.)

We can learn to speak and act respectfully no matter how mundane, difficult, or dicey the situation. By drawing on the power of the Holy Spirit to temper our tongues and guide our actions, we can speak politely and behave in a way that honors the image of God in each person we meet. This doesn't mean we don't occasionally speak hard truth. It just means we do so in an honorable way.

We can reflect the love of Jesus when we engage in conversations with a calm, collected, cheerful, civil tone. Then others might notice—as in the case of the lunch-room lady and my prank-pulling son—that our speech isn't snappy, impolite, rude, self-righteous, or snide. Our language is respectful. Our words are honoring. To those we are talking to . . . and more importantly, to God.

Will you make it your aim to speak and act respectfully and to train your children to do the same? It is a way to show love to necessary people—and everyone else!—with both our words and our demeanor.

Reflect and Deflect

My one fear in writing this book is that somehow I will give the impression that we do kind acts for others in order to be noticed. Nothing could be further from the truth! We need to remember our *why*: the reason we love and serve and give thoughtful gifts and do good works. It is so that others will see Jesus. They may *look* at us, but we hope they *see* him.

And so, when we are thanked, we thank him as well and we point others—by our words and our actions—to God. We become a mirror that reflects his image in order that others might experience his love and know his care.

And we deflect. We deflect all praise to him, the very One who allows us to live and breathe and have our being. Of course we give a gracious "You're welcome" when we are thanked, but we also make it clear the reason for our actions. We are just so grateful to God for all he has given us that we want to share our bounty with others. And we are so humbled by the love we have been shown through Jesus' death on the cross that we want to show this unconditional love to others.

Reflect and deflect. May this be not only the cry of our hearts but the utterance of our lips as well.

> *Father, thank you for all of the necessary people in my life. I admit that so many times I take them for granted. Help me to notice not only what they do but who they are as well. Give me ideas and energy that I may show them love, and keep me ever humble and continually grateful for the ways in which they help me to do life. I want to love them so that they in turn will want to love you. In Jesus' name. Amen.*

NECESSARY PEOPLE TALKING POINTS

Plumber scheduled to come calling this week? Need to take your teen to the orthodontist or your preschooler to class? Here is a list of things to do or say whenever you bump into a necessary person in your life this week. It will help to make their day a bit brighter and show your gratefulness to them for all they do.

♥ First of all, show respect for their time by honoring appointments. Be on time. In fact, be early if you can. Or, if it is your house that they will come to, write the appointment on your calendar or set a reminder on your phone. You don't want to forget about the appointment and then be out garage sale shopping when the cable guy comes. (Not that it's happened to anyone I know. Been there. Forgot that.)

♥ Engage in a little chitchat. Some necessary people work pretty lonely jobs. Interact with them and make them feel appreciated and welcome. Also, ask questions about what they do or how they came to be in the field they are in. Of course you don't want to be so inquisitive that you prevent them from performing their job. Simply ask a few questions about their vocation. Or enlist their opinion about something in a way that helps them demonstrate their knowledge and capability. Showing interest and asking questions is a way to show love.

♥ Make their job a little easier. Help bag the groceries for the store clerk. Offer to help move furniture for the carpet cleaner. Clear a path through the clutter for the furnace worker.

♥ Don't just offer a generic "thank you" when they are finished with their task. Make sure to point out something you appreciate about their work. Is your child's teacher particularly patient with a roomful of rambunctious seven-year-olds? Is your lawn care guy always cheerful, whistling away as he wields his trusty weed-whacker? Notice and then be sure to mention it to them.

CHAPTER 5

The Sick at Heart

WHAT TO SAY OR DO WHEN YOU DON'T KNOW WHAT TO SAY OR DO

What does love look like? It has the hands to help others. It has the feet to hasten to the poor and needy. It has eyes to see misery and want. It has the ears to hear the sighs and sorrows of men. That is what love looks like.
—St. Augustine

Rejoice with those who rejoice; weep with those who weep.
—Romans 12:15 (ESV)

I stood staring at the intricate, icy kaleidoscope pattern that had formed overnight on our living room picture window. Perhaps I was hoping to delay the nearly quarter-mile walk to school in the frosty February weather. Or maybe I was having one of my famous daydreams where I was starring in a Broadway musical, singing like Julie Andrews. Whatever the reason, my mother soon lit a fire under me, prodding me to get on my coat, and—more importantly—on my way.

I pulled on my plaid wool jacket and tied my scarf tightly around my face. I wriggled my toes down into my boots with the fur-trimmed tops, aided by two plastic Wonder Bread wrappers sporting their familiar red, blue, and yellow dots. Moms in the 1970s knew this slick trick to get their children's feet effortlessly into their clunky winter boots.

Before leaving, I asked my mom a question that had been on my mind. "Mom, will Lisa be back at school today?"

"I'm not sure, honey," she replied. "It may take a few more days."

My friend Lisa had just been through an awful ordeal. Her father had passed away several days earlier after a short, sudden illness. At that time in my life, I'd never known a friend whose parent had died. I was concerned for my friend and didn't know what to say or do. Later that evening, I continued my conversation with my mother. My friend hadn't shown up to school that day, and my heart began to worry even more.

I told my mother I wanted to do something nice for Lisa. While my mother appreciated my desire to reach out to my friend, she suggested that I wait a few weeks. She explained to me that when someone loses a family member, they receive lots of love, support, and attention just after the loss. But often, after a few weeks, people think the grieving should get back to their lives as normal, and sometimes the outpouring of concern and kindness dwindles. It was then, she assured me, that my friend might need me more than ever.

"You see, Karen, lots of people will bring in casseroles and flowers right now. But after a few weeks, they will stop coming. Lisa will still need her friends later when time passes but the sadness is still there. Like on their first Father's Day without their dad. Or Christmas. Or on an ordinary day when she opens the bathroom cupboard and sees his razor still sitting there. Then your friend will need encouragement too."

Lisa's father's death was my first taste of a person experiencing grief. As the years marched on, I would encounter people who experienced other types of loss—the loss of a marriage, a job, a relationship. Then the time came that I too suffered loss. First an uncle. Then a grandparent. And another grandparent. Then as an adult, a few friends. As a young married woman, I lost an unborn baby.

Most recently, I lost my sister-in-law—who was also one of my closest friends—after a two-time, decade-long battle with cancer. And I learned something about grief. It comes in waves. And often it comes out of nowhere. Even now, nearly two years after losing my sister-in-law, at times I still feel ambushed by grief.

Ambushed by Grief

This ambush often appears at unexpected times. I was waylaid recently on a random Thursday afternoon as I strolled through the culinary section of a department store. There on an end cap, I spied a springform pan. A simple short cylinder of stainless steel. That was all it took. My sister-in-law was famous for her white-chocolate raspberry cheesecake, made in her nicked and scratched, old silver springform pan. Somehow just seeing this pan reminded me that never again for a birthday or holiday would I taste her delicious dessert. I burst into tears right there in the aisle, drawing a few concerned stares from other customers nearby.

When these walls of grief suddenly close in on me, I feel as if I have nowhere to run. It is often hard to hold back my emotions. Even if I am able to do so in public, the minute I am alone, the tears trickle down my face and the memories of my loved one flood my mind.

Often I try to find ways to deal with these sudden tidal waves of sadness. I pray. Fling open my Bible to search for Scriptures, hoping something in the book of Psalms will quiet my heart. I relive memories of good times with the person I lost.

At other times, when nothing else seems to work, I lie down and drift into sleep, hoping that time out from my day to rest my mind and my soul will enable me to start anew once I wake up.

But do you know what best helps counteract these attacks of sorrow? When another person takes time from their day to reach out to me, letting me know they notice my grief.

I have been fortunate enough to experience a hand-ful of such loving gestures since my sister-in-law passed away. Sometimes it is a simple text message from a far-away friend telling me that I am on her mind today. She will add that she is praying for me as I go forward in life without my dear Thais by my side as my partner in crime. (Thais used to pull the most outrageous shenanigans, often dragging me along.) Other times I will stroll to my mailbox and discover a handwritten note from someone letting me know they are still praying for me as I adjust to my loss.

Holidays are hard. So is the week of the anniversary of her death. At each of these milestones I have received a knock on my door with a bouquet of flowers or a box of chocolate-covered strawberries. In each case, a friend sensed that this time of year would be difficult and I would be missing my sister-in-law something fierce. Each time I walked by the lovely flower arrangement or enjoyed another strawberry from the box, my sorrow softened and I felt my grief lessened by someone who took the time to remember, reach out, and love.

Sharing in the Sorrow

Romans 12:15 commands us to help ease the suffering of others: "Rejoice with those who rejoice; weep with those who weep" (ESV). We don't necessarily have to do something materially, although that certainly could be part of it. Rather, we are told to invest emotionally in the lives of others, weeping when they do. An elderly German woman at my church makes a spectacular cheesy potato and ham casserole that famously became known as "funeral potatoes" around these parts, though the dish also showed up at joyous occasions. She has often said, "A sorrow shared is but half a trouble, but joy that's shared is a joy made double."

This concept is so true! Who doesn't like to celebrate joys and successes with others? It certainly makes them more fun. And we look forward to celebrating when a friend or family member has a reason to rejoice. Maybe we don't love the long drive to the wedding, but we certainly love to share in the celebration: the food, the dancing, the merriment. (And those pastel melt-away mints! Yum!)

But sharing in the sorrow of another person is a little more trying. Even though we know it is the right—and biblical—thing to do, it can be awkward. We don't know what to say. How to say it. Or even if we should say anything at all. We aren't always sure if the grieving person will want us around. Though our hearts may mean well, our hands, feet, and mouths are sometimes at a loss as to what to do.

Even though I am able to recall times when someone's sentiments or heartfelt touch eased my grief, I still find myself debating what to say and do at times like these. So I decided to reach out and ask my blog readers what they feel is most appropriate and helpful at a loss of a loved one, a divorce, or other such tragedy. Here are some of their very wise words.

Marilyn wrote: "When my husband and I miscarried our second child, some good friends of ours called and told us they were taking us out to dinner. Of course, it was the last thing we wanted to do, but they came to our house, picked us up, and drove us to the restaurant. We had pizza. They just sat with us quietly. If we spoke, they engaged in the conversation; if we laughed, they laughed with us; and when we cried, they gently and lovingly held us. It meant so much that they never pressured us to feel a certain way. They were just available to us in our great grief."

Another reader, Anna, felt comfort when her friends shared verses from God's Word during a time of grief. She tries to do the same when she is comforting someone. "It's so meaningful when someone looks up specific verses to comfort you about exactly what you are going through. I usually try to frame or laminate the verses I choose so they can hang them in their house where they will see them. It's a very small thing, but his Word brings the most comfort. I have also handwritten notes of encouragement or prayers letting the person know that I am thinking of and praying for them and what they are going through."

Many times, we want to alert the suffering person to our ability and desire to help. So we mumble something like, "If there is anything you need or something I can do, please let me know." We mean well. And we mean what we say. But many readers stressed that this really isn't helpful. Aimee wrote: "Don't say, 'Let me know if you need anything.' When you're going through a difficult time, the last thing you'll have energy for is (1) figuring out what you need, and (2) picking up the phone to ask. Show up, take over a task, and allow the person to concentrate on what they need to. I spent my dad's final four months by his side. We have five kids, and our nephew joined our family in that time. My husband literally became mom and dad for the days I was gone. Friends showed up and took my kids to their commitments, cooked for us, picked up my kids for playdates, took my daughter shopping for a new dress for her Papa's funeral, and so on. There was never a 'what can I do to help?' Friends simply showed up and did what needed to be done."

My good friend Tammy, who has been through many episodes of grief and deals with the ongoing challenge of raising an adult son with Down syndrome, shared this: "I've had different kinds of grief. The loss of our babies, the loss of my parents, the grief of Jacob's disability. Each one is a little different, but in every case, I have needed people who will just be there to listen. People who let me feel all the emotions I was experiencing. If you're trying to help someone, don't just throw Bible verses out there and say, 'God has it all under control.' I know that, but at the moment I am broken. I need your compassion and grace. You don't have to fix me; just let me know I'm not alone in this. I needed people who stopped by with coffee and food. Sent a card or a text message. Three ladies actually decorated my Christmas tree and wrapped my presents one year, and that was priceless. One of my best friends helped me do the picture boards for both of my parents' funerals. It was so nice to be able to talk about the pictures and my memories. And that brings me to this: don't act like nothing happened (if it's a tragic death or, like me, losing two babies due to tubal pregnancies).

You don't have to say anything. Give me a hug and say nothing."

And finally, Dominique felt that although meals and practical help were good, she too found that the best thing to do was to simply sit there and listen. She urged, "Say nothing. Sometimes, you just sitting there and allowing me to cry or listen to me vent is weirdly comforting. Advice or words just to fill the space isn't necessary."

Reading the comments on my site opened my eyes and gave me ideas of what to do and what *not* to do. But perhaps the thing I learned the most is to be honest. Don't be shy about your desire to help and love or about your ignorance of what is best to say or do. Simply tell them that you love them. That you can't imagine what they are feeling, but you want to share their pain. You want to lighten their load. Or you want to simply sit there in the pain with them to let them know you care.

Make a point to ask God how you should proceed. Should you call and check on them periodically? Should you show up unannounced? Should you just take over the household chores and responsibilities for a while so they can properly grieve? Be clear and considerate as you relay your desire to be helpful without being annoying, to be loving without being too loud. To help bear their burden during their time of sadness.

Heartache at the Holidays

Remember to be especially sensitive to the grieving during the holidays. It can be sheer torture for a person or family still heart-deep in grief to watch the rest of the world smiling with sleigh bells ringing and lights twinkling.

In 2013, Pastor Rick and Kay Warren lost their adult son Matthew to suicide. When Christmastime rolled around, it was hard for Kay to open the many Christmas cards that flooded her mailbox each day in December, showcasing seemingly perfect families living joyous lives. Then the day came when this daily duty of opening the mail became too much for her.

Kay wrote:

The cards remained unopened in the traditional iron sleigh that has held our cards through the years until after Christmas Day had passed. Weeks later, I tore through them, angry tears pouring down my cheeks as I separated them into three piles: ones that didn't mention our grief, ones that did so with a short, "Praying for you," and ones that included soothing, loving, and thoughtful words of compassion and empathy. The third stack was the smallest.

Recently I opened the first Christmas card of this season. I wondered if perhaps I had been oversensitive last December—so immersed in our family's loss at the time that every expression of happiness was like scraping an open wound. I hoped that I'd feel differently this holiday season. When I opened the card—an artfully designed print on heavy paper stock, printed with a signature from a pastor I don't even know—I threw it away.

Last week I wrote about this experience on Facebook. I asked readers to consider sending a plain card to grieving families (instead of an obligatory "happy family" photo). "Tell them in a few words that you are aware of how painful Christmas can be and that you are praying for them," I wrote. "Yes, it's inconvenient—it will take more time than your rushed signature, and it will require entering into someone else's loss, mourning, grief, and anger."[2]

One Christmas about ten years ago I learned first-hand how painful the holiday can be for those who are mourning.

"It's the most wonderful time of the year!" The loud-speaker blared the joyful lyrics of the familiar song that snowy Christmas Eve afternoon.

Everywhere I looked, people were searching for last-minute gift purchases, holiday baking ingredients, or that one final string of twinkle lights that would make their Christmas downright Norman Rockwell perfect.

As I stood in line paying for the ingredients for my assigned cheesy potato casserole for our family gathering, a lump formed in my throat. Soon my lips quivered and hot tears fell onto my wind-chapped cheeks.

How could everyone be so happy? Why was the world going on as if nothing had happened? My friend Julie had died the night before, leaving behind a husband and eight children who needed her. Didn't anyone care?

I wanted to scream. I wanted the holidays to be canceled that year. There was no cheer in me, and I thought the rest of the world should follow suit and just "hum-bug" the whole celebration.

Although our hearts were heavy, our family tried to make the most of Christmas, especially for our children, who were sad about their friends' mother's death. Over the next few months, my husband and I carried on with our normal life and tried to help our widowed friend as best we could.

Several in our circle of friends made meals on a weekly basis. A college girl offered to clean their home. One of Julie's sons joined our homeschool for kindergarten a few days each week. Although we still experienced great heartache knowing our friend wasn't coming back, lightening her husband's load and being there for the children made us feel we were fulfilling the mission God had for us.

Ever since that year, our family has become more aware of the fact that for many, Thanksgiving and Christmas aren't the most wonderful times of the year. Loneliness looms. Depressions darken. While scores of us delight in the season, drinking in the sights, sounds, and smells, others are numb from pain.

A neighbor of mine had a good perspective on helping those who hurt. She once told me, "The holidays are an excuse for making someone's life better." She was right! There are people waiting to be encouraged and included during the holidays. If only we would cease our own sometimes self-focused hustle and bustle long enough to see!

After that sad season in our family's life, we've made it our mission to reach out at the holidays instead of playing the commercialized "gimmee game." Thanksgiving and Christmas are not about getting. The very essence of both is giving.

When our family has been intentional about being Jesus' hands and feet at the holidays, he has allowed us to brighten the lives of many. We get to show his love and character expressed in Psalm 68:5–6: "A father to the fatherless, a defender of widows, is God in his holy dwelling. God sets the lonely in families."

Others are welcomed at our table. We sing Christmas carols to shut-ins, decorate homes and address Christmas cards for widows, shop for the needy, bake for the brokenhearted, and often include the lonely in our normal holiday activities as if they were part of our family. Because really, they are.

What We Learn from Ruth

The Bible includes many stories of close relationships. David and Jonathan. Jesus and John. Barnabas and Paul. But the relationship I admire most is the one between a woman and her mother-in-law. Yes. You read that right. That female-to-female relationship that is often the butt of jokes—my personal favorite being, "Do you know that if you rearrange the letters in 'mother-in-law,' you come up with 'Woman Hitler'?"

Sorry. Couldn't resist.

But there was no such strain in the relationship between Ruth and Naomi. In fact, what could have been a setup for extreme tension became an avenue for tenderness instead.

Ruth was a Moabite. Because of her nationality, she was not a member of God's chosen people, Israel. But that did not prevent her from loving and following the one true God.

During the time of the judges, a famine swept over Israel. Looking for food, one family moved to the country of Moab, not far away: a man named Elimelek, his wife Naomi, and their sons Mahlon and Kilion. After Elimilek died, his sons married women from Moab. One of the women, Ruth, became Mrs. Mahlon. About ten years into their marriage, Mahlon passed away too. Ruth, who had become a convert to Yahweh worship, accompanied her mother-in-law back to Bethlehem, willingly leaving her homeland to care for her widowed mother-in-law.

One of the Bible's most famous verses is in the book of Ruth. Although the verse speaks to the relationship of Ruth and Naomi, it showed up at a certain ceremony in 1986 when a bride wrote and recited her own vows to her foxy husband standing in his ivory long-tailed tux. (I wonder who?) Ruth 1:16 reads, "Where you go I will go, and where you stay I will stay. Your people will be my people and your God my God."

Although she was dealing with grief herself, Ruth stuck by her mother-in-law. She was loyal. And compassionate. She decided to keep doing life with Naomi, and God rewarded her for it. What can we learn from the story of Ruth that might help us today as we interact with those who are sorrowful?

FIRST, PUT OTHERS' WISHES AHEAD OF YOUR OWN.

I love how in this story, each woman desired what was best for the other. Naomi felt her daughter-in-law should stay in her own country, among her own people, and so she was prepared to hop on the bus back to Bethlehem without Ruth. But Ruth wouldn't hear of it! Perhaps worried about a woman Naomi's age traveling and living alone, Ruth insisted that she would relocate to a foreign land. Ruth put Naomi's needs above her own.

Today, we can adopt this principle when dealing with those who are sorrowful. Maybe we would love to celebrate Thanksgiving with just the members of our own sweet family, eating our familiar foods and playing a cutthroat game of Pit or Flinch (which is how we Ehmans roll). Down the street, however, lives a widow facing her first Thanksgiving without her husband and without any other relatives nearby. Could your family make room at the table for her, putting her needs above your desires?

Or how about this scenario? You would love nothing more this weekend than a quiet Saturday morning all to yourself. But you know that a friend across town is living with the fallout of a recent divorce—and for her, the Saturday morning quiet is deafening. Could you kidnap her for the morning, take her out for coffee and a muffin, and engage in some heartfelt conversation? It will not only encourage her, but you will be blessed as well.

NEXT, GO WITH THEM.

Ruth made a drastic life change when she decided to travel with Naomi to Bethlehem. A change of physical address may not be necessary for us when we help a friend, but sometimes we do need to change where our thoughts and hearts dwell. We need to learn to see beyond ourselves and our lives and into the pain of others. We must make this a matter of prayer, asking God to increase our sensitivity to what others are thinking and feeling. How will they feel at the next family function? What are they thinking as they sit on the sidelines of the baseball game? When milestones or holidays approach, do their hearts migrate to a place of sorrow? Ask God to break your heart with what breaks theirs. Then ask him to show you what you can do in a tangible way to let them know that your thoughts and prayers are with them. We need to push past our comfortable life and climb into the skin of others who are grieving, so we know best how to minister to them. We need to go with them to their mournful place.

MAKE THEIR PEOPLE YOUR PEOPLE.

As a person moves through the various stages of grief, sometimes he or she has no emotional energy left to deal with even the most basic tasks of life. This is a particular challenge for a parent, since their children need them to be available physically and emotionally. So many of my blog readers who responded to my query about what helped them during grief said that those who stepped in to care for their children and loved ones were a treasure.

Perhaps you can take over the carpool duties for your grieving friend. Can you go to her house and play with her young children while she takes a nap? Can you help her address Christmas cards or shop for birthday gifts when she just doesn't have the energy?

You may also be able to be a sounding board for children or other loved ones when a grieving person doesn't have the emotional strength to do so. I remember when my grandmother died when I was in the fourth grade. I knew my mother was very sad, and even at that young age I could sense she didn't feel like talking or answering my questions. Instead, I sat on my Aunt Patty's lap while she brushed the tangles out of my hair and talked with her about my grandmother and her death.

FINALLY, ALLOW YOUR GOD TO BE THEIR GOD SO THEY CAN WITNESS YOUR FAITH UP CLOSE.

Throughout the book of Ruth we see the relationship of Ruth and Naomi deepen. They go from being strangers to relatives to close friends at heart. It seems that God was at the center of their relationship and communication. Through her mother-in-law, Ruth got to know the God of Israel, seeing him as she watched Naomi live through both the joyous and troublesome times.

Do you make it a point to bring God into your relationships? Do you allow others to hear you talk about him? Do you share your doubts and hopes and quiet thoughts about a relationship with him? When we make it a point to be open about our relationship with God, it deepens our friendships. Then in times of grief, we are able to respond with greater intimacy and empathy because we have connected previously on a spiritual level.

─────── **The Power of a Pause** ───────

Grief does not go away quickly. Often people carry its weight for years, even decades. When we listen for their heart drops, we can purpose to show them love and help to lighten their load. And not just one time. But many, many times, in ways both mundane and magical.

We recently experienced this in our own family. My son has a friend who hangs out at our house—and eats lots of our food! He lived mainly with his dad, but his paternal grandmother was also very involved in raising him. When he was in middle school, she was diagnosed with an aggressive cancer that soon took her life. Whenever he talks about his grandmother, there is still a twinge of sorrow in his voice.

One day as we were discussing his grandmother, this teenager started to talk about her cooking. I asked him his favorite thing that she used to make. "That's easy," he answered. "Double-meat lasagna and pineapple upside-down cake." I listened to him describe how delicious these two dishes had been. And then I walked into the other room, and I wrote down his answer in the Notes app on my cell phone.

A few days before he was to move away to attend college, we had this young man and his father over for dinner. I bet you can guess what was on the menu that night. Yup. Double-meat lasagna and pineapple upside-down cake.

When I called everyone to the table and he saw what I had prepared, he choked up. He gave me a big hug and quickly sat down and devoured his dinner. Yes, he had eaten at our table many times before. But this night was magical. After we had eaten, I assured this young man that his grandmother would be so proud of who he had become. And since she wasn't around anymore to cook his favorite meal for him as a send-off to college, I decided I would step in and have the honor of doing so.

Now let me assure you that I didn't carry out this quest without a little struggle. It came on a week where I was slammed. I was tempted to just order pizza and have ice cream for dessert, but I knew how much a home-cooked meal like his grandmother used to make would mean to this boy. And the pause and the preparation were good for my soul. They reminded me that relationships require work, that remembering isn't always easy—and that sometimes sweat is involved in listening and loving.

As we go through life this week, may we be ever aware of those around us who are grieving—for a friend, a loved one, a marriage, a job, or a relationship. May we seek to weep with them, reaching out to help carry their load. When we do, we fulfill the law of Christ.

Whose load will you help carry this week?

Dear Lord, show me how to share your love with someone who is sick at heart and sorrowful. Help me listen to their grief, lessen their pain, and lighten their load. I want to be your heart and hands and feet. In Jesus' name. Amen.

GOOD GRIEF

Here are five points to keep in mind as you interact with those who are sick at heart:

G—Give them space. Don't expect them to bounce right back after a few weeks and act like their old selves. The grief process takes a long time, and people will continue to miss a loved one until the day they die. Be consistent in reaching out to them, including them, and showing them love. Do not be offended if they don't consistently act like their old selves. They need a little space and a lot of time.

R—Remember their loved one out loud. Don't be afraid to speak of the one who has passed away or their loved one who is suffering from a disease. It usually makes it worse when no one will mention the name of the deceased. When you feel it is appropriate, talk about their loved one, mentioning a happy memory or funny story or one of their character qualities. Keep their memory alive in your conversations. A friend who lost his son in the Iraq war once told me, "Don't be afraid to speak his name. Speaking his name doesn't remind me that my son died. I know he died. Speaking his name reminds me that you remember that he lived."

I—Invite them along. Even though the grieving need space, they still need to know that you want to include them in your activities. Make it a point to invite them out to lunch or to take in a movie or show. Ask them to take in a sporting event or a concert. Don't be offended if they aren't up to going. Just keep inviting them, so they know you care.

E—Etch important dates on your calendar. Holidays and other special dates are especially hard the first few years— Christmas, birthdays, Mother's or Father's Day. Make plans to reach out to the grieving on these difficult occasions. Did your friends lose their son in his senior year of high school? Make sure to send a thoughtful card during graduation time in the spring, letting them know you are praying for them. Did your neighbor lose her husband to a heart attack? Find out their wedding anniversary and offer to take your neighbor out for coffee or lunch. One of my favorite ideas was when my young boys took flowers to a sweet older widow on what would have been her wedding anniversary. We told her that since Grandpa Don was busy in heaven, he had us deliver the love that day.

F—Frame a favorite picture. Print a photo of the person and their loved one who is now gone. It is a simple gift but one that will be appreciated. When my sister-in-law passed away, my friend Mandy purchased a small Christmas ornament that framed a picture of my sister-in-law. Each Christmas when we hang it on the tree, I fondly remember not only my relative but my thoughtful friend.

CHAPTER 6

Chipped Crock-Pots and Stained Carpets

LIVING A LIFE OF WELCOME

The ornaments of your house will be the guests who frequent it.

—AUTHOR UNKNOWN

All the believers were one in heart and mind. No one claimed that any of their possessions was their own, but they shared everything they had.

—ACTS 4:32

On the second Sunday of October during our senior year in college, my boyfriend popped the question and slipped a heart-shaped diamond ring on my finger. I was ecstatic. Not only was I looking forward to becoming

Mrs. Todd Ehman, but I was also eagerly anticipating setting up our very first apartment, complete with all things decorative, domestic, and culinary. And of course the very first step was filling out the bridal registry at the local JC Penney department store.

Now, while I was giddy that Saturday morning as I dragged my new fiancé to the mall, he was less than thrilled. Oh, he tried to feign interest, but after about forty-five minutes of "Do you think we should pick the seafoam-green bathroom towels or do you prefer the pacific-blue shade instead?" he'd had it. He parked himself on the edge of a nearby display, completely exasperated, and finally uttered, "You know what? I really don't have any preference about all of this. You decide."

That admission might have upset other girls who longed for a picture-perfect day of planning with their soon-to-be husband, but being somewhat of a control freak, I was actually relieved. This gave me complete freedom to single-handedly choose the countless items I wanted for our tiny, 400-square-foot apartment in the woods that we would call our first home. And so choose I did.

Two muffin tins, one nonstick cookie sheet, six peach washcloths, and two ivory bath towels. A Crock-Pot. A crystal vase. Ivory lace fingertip guest towels for the bathroom. And on it went, seven pages' worth of domestic bliss.

My vision of a quaint and charming little apartment was coming together beautifully. And my fiancé was rewarded for his patience with a trip to our favorite sandwich shop, T. E. Murch's, to order a turkey and Swiss, heavy on the mayo, and sprinkled with alfalfa sprouts, just the way he likes it. All in all it was a good day, and remembering it invokes feelings of sweet nostalgia in my soul.

In reality, though, I wish I were able to travel back in time and reselect my household items, this time with two decades of perspective and a little more practicality. Here's how it would all go down:

Instead of debating between the Crock-Pot with the light-peach hearts on it or the one with the country-blue ducks and geese (Hey! Don't judge. It was the 1980s and peach hearts and country-blue ducks and geese were all the rage), instead I would choose black. And chip resistant. After all, the Crock-Pot would have to stand up to decades of beef stew for a crowd and overnight oatmeal for the half-dozen football players who stayed each Saturday during gridiron season. When the black Crock-Pot did chip, I could take a Sharpie marker and make it look new again. Well. Sorta new. At least not noticeably nicked.

Then we have the household linens. I would probably opt out of the ivory-and-peach color scheme. Instead, towels for the guest bathroom would be in the preferred and also practical shade of dirt brown or muddy tan. That way, when my children's friends spent the night after a day at the playground or a weekend tournament up at the baseball fields, I wouldn't stress so much about getting stains out of ivory towels and peach-colored washcloths.

And then that lone nonstick cookie sheet. This single piece of kitchen equipment was hardly prepared for what lay ahead. Baking six-dozen cookies for the cookie exchange at church. Making enough homemade stuffed-crust pizzas to feed my daughter's thirteen-year-old friends at her slumber party. Or whipping up enough oatmeal monster cookies to send with the football team as they headed off to summer training camp. I should've opted for a half-dozen of the industrial size, commercial-grade stainless steel ones instead.

Finally, a crystal vase? What was I thinking? I should have had no glass, pottery, or crystal in my decorating scheme. At least not out in the main living areas. Metal vases, wooden bowls, and sturdy woven baskets would be best. These are less likely to get damaged during an airsoft gun war or a hearty game of Nerf basketball on a rainy day.

Living a life of welcome—opening both your heart and your home—means your stuff gets used. And reused. Over and over again. Your items get nicked and scratched. Your carpet and rugs and linens get stained. While this doesn't mean we don't try to make our surroundings pleasant, it does mean we learn to accept some degree of imperfection. Well-used items often mean that we have loved well.

Who Owns Your Stuff?

Our culture values ownership. We cannot wait to own our first car. Then our first home. Often we accumulate other items that indicate we have "arrived." Perhaps a snowmobile. A Jet Ski. A second home in the form of a cottage up north on a lake. Even children and teenagers want to own the latest gadget or gizmo. We think that owning these objects will make us happy. But who really owns our stuff?

In 1 Chronicles 29, we see King David preparing to build God's temple. He mentions how he will spare no resource on the construction but will give out of his own possessions and personal treasures of gold and silver. Then, without being asked, other Israelite leaders join in too, willingly and joyfully donating gold, silver, bronze, iron, and precious jewels to the building fund (see 1 Chronicles 29:6–9).

After the resources are gathered for the temple, David praises God in front of the whole assembly. Notice that he doesn't praise the people for their generosity nor boast about himself and his charitable giving. No. Study his words carefully, especially the phrases I have emphasized below.

> David praised the LORD in the presence of the whole assembly, saying,
>
> "Praise be to you, LORD, the God of our father Israel, from everlasting to everlasting. Yours, LORD, is the greatness and the power and the glory and the majesty and the splendor, *for everything in heaven and earth is yours.* Yours, LORD, is the kingdom; you are exalted as head over all. *Wealth and honor come from you*; you are the ruler of all things. In your hands are strength and power to exalt and give strength to all.

"Now, our God, we give you thanks, and praise your glorious name.

"But who am I, and who are my people, that we should be able to give as generously as this? *Everything comes from you, and we have given you only what comes from your hand.* We are foreigners and strangers in your sight, as were all our ancestors. Our days on earth are like a shadow, without hope. LORD *our God, all this abundance that we have provided for building you a temple for your Holy Name comes from your hand, and all of it belongs to you.* I know, my God, that you test the heart and are pleased with integrity. All these things I have given willingly and with honest intent. And now I have seen with joy how willingly your people who are here have given to you." (1 Chronicles 29:10–17, emphasis added)

Wow.

Everything comes from you, and we have given you only what comes from your hand.

What an amazing perspective on our possessions. If the ancient Israelites were so willing to offer up what God had given them, turning right back around and investing in building his temple, could we today use all that he has given us to build up the church and encourage others who might not know him yet? It is a subtle but crucial shift in perspective when we realize that all the material items we have worked for here on Earth really do not belong to us. Instead they all come from the hand of God. They are his in the first place, and they are his at the end of our lives. The question comes down to this: who owns your stuff?

When I have the mindset that David has as he prays to God in front of the assembly, it makes it easier when my stuff gets stained. When my trinkets get tarnished. When my belongings get broken. Even those beautiful handpicked ones I asked for on our bridal registry. After all, they really don't belong to me. They are God's. What happens to them while they are being used here on Earth to build his kingdom is not my concern. My concern should be with my attitude toward using these things to reach out to others.

How to Make Your Home a Haven

When we have a God-honoring perspective about our possessions and resources, our hearts and homes can become a wheelhouse for ministry. We can lead with our hearts and bless with our homes, making our homes a haven not only for those who dwell there permanently but for whoever God sends our way. And believe me, he will send people your way. As I look back over two decades of married life, I see many times that God has used our home as a haven for others—first in our tiny apartment and now in our average-size home as a family of five.

During the early years when we lived in a small apartment, I was a substitute teacher and cheerleading coach and Todd was a youth pastor. For the first five years of our marriage we did not have any children of our own, but teenagers often filled our home. Sometimes a cheerleader from my squad needed to talk through something, perhaps an issue involving her school friends or turmoil at home with her family. I learned to have soft drinks on hand and snacks in the cupboard, ready to serve as I sat down and listened.

Other times, we opened our home as part of a planned get-together for the teenagers in our youth group. Though our very first home sported a tiny living room, teens sprawled on the floor or piled on the couch and love seat, listening to my husband give a Bible lesson or just watching a sporting event on TV. Sure, soda got spilled and cheese puffs were ground into the carpet, but we knew that truth was being shared and life lessons were being cemented in the hearts and minds of those teenagers. These young people who God brought our way felt our home was a safe place where they could speak about their lives and not be judged. While our home was nothing like the pages of an interior design magazine, to these teens, it was beautiful.

As we grew older and became parents ourselves, the children inside our four walls changed. Now it was a group of toddlers for a playdate or a bunch of Little Leaguers after their championship win. A few years later, once again teenagers were our frequent guests; this time they were our children's friends. Today, although teenagers are our most frequent guests, young adults also drop over, the friends of our oldest two. Most of them are married and some even have children of their own. The members of our small group at church also gather to meet on Sunday afternoons.

Our aim is the same for all of these guests. We don't offer hospitality to them in order to impress them with our home or our food or our decorating prowess. Instead, we want to refresh them. To give them a place where they can relax and unwind. To provide a setting where they can talk and question and contemplate. Most of all, we offer our home to God to be used as a ministry tool in building his kingdom-temple here on earth.

To be sure, all these guests have made their mark, and not always in a good way! We have had our brand new picnic table scribbled on with permanent marker. Our carpet stained with grape soda. Glasses dropped and shattered. A pizza stone cracked in two. Once-new towels are now threadbare and ragged. My wood furniture shows a white ring from a guest who left out a glass of iced tea overnight.

But along with all the destruction of property came work for God's kingdom. The gospel was woven into conversations with others. Babies were rocked as I watched them and gave their weary moms a break. Teens were encouraged when they failed to make the team or land the part in the play. The Bible was studied and questioned and believed. Tummies were fed. Hearts were filled.

When we willingly open our homes, we aren't just being nice. We are being obedient to God's Word. First Peter 4:8–10 states,

> Above all, love each other deeply, because love covers over a multitude of sins. Offer hospitality to one another without grumbling. Each of you should use whatever gift you have received to serve others, as faithful stewards of God's grace in its various forms.

We are doing exactly what God expects us to do when we offer hospitality. Without grumbling. Or fretting over our broken and soiled stuff or our "too small" home. If there is room in your heart, you'll make room in your home.

If you long to open your home—and your heart—to be used by God, you must be ready. Here are some tips for doing both, so that others can feel your place is a safe haven and can sense the love of Jesus there.

PREPARE YOUR HEART.

Before you begin to prepare your home for planned guests or impromptu company, you first must prepare your heart. Each morning ask God to help you to have a willing and hospitable spirit toward whomever he sends your way. Pray that he will direct your time spent in the Scriptures to specific verses you may use to comfort or encourage others as you visit with them in your home. Ask him to soften your heart and remove any sense of exclusive ownership over your possessions. Cultivate the perspective that David had: *everything comes from God.* Then be prepared to use what God has given you to bless and strengthen others.

PREPARE YOUR HOME.

Think about your home and the guests who might visit. How can you best prepare your home for the people who might stop over? Perhaps your children are all past the toddler stage, but you and your husband are teaching a young married class at church. In what ways could you make your home child-friendly for those sweet young families who might come over for a meal or snack?

Even before we had children, the corner in our living room housed a large, round market basket I found at a garage sale. Inside the basket were all kinds of baby and toddler toys I'd picked up at yard sales and secondhand stores. This way, whenever someone stopped by who had a young child, they could choose something from the basket to keep the little one occupied while we visited. After we purchased a home that had a stairway, we also kept a safety gate in the closet. This helped young parents to relax and visit with us rather than worry that their child was going to wander from the living room into the kitchen and tumble down the basement stairs. And it isn't just the young that we should be concerned about. Will you have elderly folks over to visit sometimes? Think through what you might be able to do to make your home a comfortable place for them, barrier-free and safe.

STOCK THE PANTRY.

We don't have to be super organized in order to be hospitable. We just have to be prepared. We need to recognize that during this season of life, we may have drop-in guests, and so we need to prepare in advance for those times when the doorbell rings. So let's think for a moment about our pantry. Does it hold the necessary components to whip up a dinner should company arrive unexpectedly? Or is it more like Old Mother Hubbard's, bare and lacking anything that could be used to feed your guests?

You don't want to serve your guests a substandard meal like "helper." You know. When you don't even have any hamburger, so you are forced to serve them just the helper. Trust me. Guests don't normally like helper. (Although they probably will smile and rave about its uniqueness.) Make sure your pantry contains staple items you could serve to guests: coffee, tea, snack crackers, rice or pasta that would make a quick side dish, chips and salsa, canned soup to go with a simple sandwich, tuna fish to make tuna melts for an easy lunch, and so on. But it isn't just the dry goods we need to think about. Review my tips in chapter three about filling your freezer!

ROLL OUT THE WELCOME MAT.

Make sure that people know your door is open. Of course there will be times that it is inconvenient for you to have guests at the drop of a hat, but do let those in your life know that should they desire to visit or talk something through, you are more than happy to have them over as long as it works for your family. Be sincere. Give them your cell phone number and tell them to text you if they would like to stop by. I think back on my own life, especially when I was a teenager and a new Christian. A few women were always willing to allow me to stop by for a surprise visit. Their hearts and pantries and homes were open. Through them I became a disciple over a taco salad or bowl of chili. One woman, the wife of my youth pastor, always seemed to have the makings for taco salad in her house and could feed a half-dozen teenagers with only about fifteen minutes' notice. To this day, any time I eat taco salad, I think of her.

LEAN IN AND LISTEN.

When we make our home a respite for others, we shouldn't jump too quickly to giving unsolicited advice. We need to learn to listen. To allow others to share what's on their hearts as we pray and ponder what we will say *if* they directly ask for our advice. We need to learn to listen between the lines for any deeper issues they might be not sharing. Our goal should not be to fix other people but to listen and to love and to leave the fixing up to God.

REFRAIN FROM PREACHING.

Let's be careful not to make our living room our pulpit. As others open up to us about their struggles in life, we must refrain from preaching. Of course we want to speak God's truth and to have his Word saturate our conversation. Of course we need to be ready and willing to share the gospel with them, telling them of Jesus and how he purchased their salvation on the cross, but we must not wag our fingers. Sometimes in our zeal to inspire others, we come across as judgmental. I love to think of the way Jesus interacted with sinners. He spoke truth. He called them to sin no more. But he was full of compassion and mercy and gentleness. God calls us to take the same approach.

PERFECT THE ART OF FOLLOW-UP.

Once others have been inside our homes and have shared their hearts with us, we have the opportunity to follow up with them. Text them a few days later to see how they are doing. Drop a note in the mail to tell them you are praying for them. Hop on their Facebook page and thank them for the great visit. Continue to keep the door open to your home and the avenue for conversation accessible to them. Keeping your relationship intact and looking for opportunities to spend time together can be a great way to love and care for them.

— "Home": An Attitude, Not Always a House —

Although I've been focusing on the home, hospitality doesn't just happen within the confines of those four walls. You can be hospitable wherever you are!

Think of your office. Is it designed to impress and intimidate, or is it inviting, with an atmosphere of an open door, an open heart, and maybe a dish of candy for those who stop by?

What about your vehicle—especially if you are schlepping kids around to sports and activities? Is it stocked with tissues, healthy snacks, and a relatively clean interior? Do your kids' friends feel welcome when they climb inside? Make it your habit to ask them about their day and be interested in their lives. Your car or van can become a welcoming place as you cart your crew around.

How about your possessions—your land or recreational vehicles or even simple, everyday items? Do you share with others rather than keeping it all to yourself? We've been blessed by friends who let our deer-and rabbit-hunting boys set up a tree stand on their acreage during hunting season. Do you own a pool? Perhaps you could let a friend use it to host their child's birthday party.

Anything else you can willingly share—a trampoline, boat, trailer, tent, snowmobile, or other grown-up "toys"?

Even simple things such as books, videos, and CDs can be shared, bonding you and the recipient. The first believers in the early church set a wonderful standard for us to follow: "No one claimed that any of their possessions was their own, but they shared everything they had" (Acts 4:32). Whether you share a book or a bicycle, a cot or a cottage, do it with an attitude of openhandedness and openheartedness, sharing with others what God has given to you.

Enjoying the town where you live is also a great way to be hospitable. Book a dinner at a restaurant you know your friends will enjoy and then treat them by picking up the tab. Attend a local sporting event or concert together and then take your friend out for dessert and coffee. Picnic dinners at a beach or park can be wonderful ways to offer hospitality and encourage others without actually utilizing your home.

— Throw Another Cup of Water in the Soup —

When I was a young girl, people seemed more willing to stretch whatever food they had and welcome others to their table. I often heard people of my mother's generation say how their parents—who lived through the Depression—simply used to throw another few cups of water in the soup to make it stretch further when company dropped by. But today, in a culture saturated with Pinterest images of perfection that showcase lovely tablescapes, stunning décor, and gourmet fare, we aren't so willing to have others into our home to break bread or share a plate of nachos. What has happened? We have mixed up the notions of entertaining and offering hospitality.

Entertaining puts the emphasis on you and your home and seeks to impress others. In contrast, hospitality puts the emphasis on your guest and seeks to help them to feel refreshed, not impressed, when they leave your home. When I think back on my life and the people whose hospitality I've enjoyed, what comes to my mind most often is not the food they served but the attitude with which they served it. They were welcoming. Interested in my life. Concerned for my comfort. In most of the circumstances, I couldn't even tell you what was on the menu that day. What I enjoyed most, and what I carried with me for years, was the feeling of love and acceptance I received when I was around these people, inside their homes.

Think of those in your life today. Would they say that your home was a safe place—a haven for them when they were stressed or troubled? Will you pray and prepare, both your heart and your home, to be a part of God's plan in their lives? Will you adopt a perspective that all we have been given—from our home to our car and everything else—belongs to God and is given to us to share with others?

Get ready. I think I hear a knock on the door. Time to throw another cup of water in the soup. Or to grab another soul and head out for a cup of cheer. Anything to share love with another person in your life.

Father, may I be ever mindful that all I have belongs to you. Help me to lean in and listen this week, seeking to cheer a weary soul or offer welcome to one who needs to know your love. I want my heart and home to be open as I serve you by loving others. In Jesus' name. Amen.

IDEAS FOR COOKING FOR A CROWD

Company's coming? Don't fret. Here are a few helpful tips and some easy menu ideas.

♥ **Number one rule.** Do *not* try a new recipe out on company. Stick to the ones you have tested that have turned out well. Been there. Burnt that.

♥ **Don't try to be fancy.** Gourmet food isn't necessary. Try instead to stick to this guideline: serve simple foods but plenty of them. Better a hearty meatloaf and mashed potatoes with enough to go around than a small fancy casserole that includes ingredients no one has heard of and is rather skimpy, so folks feel they can't take a heaping helping.

♥ **Inquire about allergies or sensitivities.** Be sure to check with guests to see if anyone has any allergies or sensitivities to any foods, and then plan your menus accordingly.

And now, some ideas of what to serve:

♥ **Baked potato bar:** Bake up several large potatoes (russets work best) and then serve them with various toppings, such as chopped ham, crumbled bacon, sautéed mushrooms and onions, cheddar cheese, blue cheese, cooked broccoli, or prepared chili, in addition to the standard butter and sour cream. To create a theme, also serve root beer floats so you can call it "Suds and Spuds Night."

♥ **Build your own burger.** Make it a retro diner night! Bake up a big batch of French fries in the oven as you grill hamburgers on the grill. Provide buns and various toppings: sliced cheese, lettuce, tomatoes, onions, jalapeños, and so on. Serve milk shakes to go with them. Don't forget the whipped cream and cherries on top.

♥ **Host a soup and salad luncheon.** You don't have to make all the food. Guests are usually more than happy to help out with the cuisine while you provide the place for a get-together. Hold a soup and salad buffet potluck. Guests bring either a cold salad or a hot Crock-Pot of soup to share. You provide bread or rolls and butter.

♥ **Old-fashioned ice cream or pie social.** This idea is inspired by friends who always hosted an ice cream social on June 21, the longest day of the year. Simply have all your guests bring a topping for the ice cream: chocolate, caramel, butterscotch, chocolate chips, hot fudge, strawberries, raspberries, peaches, bananas, chopped nuts, sprinkles, or whipped cream. You provide gallons of ice cream and table service. Everyone can craft their own sundae and enjoy visiting as they eat. Or make it a pie social, inviting everyone to bring a pie to share. You provide the ice cream to go on top!

CHAPTER 7

The Lonely and Unloved

HOW TO BE THEIR FAMILY AND BLESS YOURS TOO

The most terrible poverty is loneliness, and the feeling of being unloved.
—MOTHER TERESA

God sets the lonely in families.
—PSALM 68:6

One of the most memorable people I ever met was a scrawny eight-year-old boy who lived on the street near our apartment complex when Todd and I were newly married. Usually dressed in his green and tan T-Rex dinosaur costume left over from Halloween, he could often be found riding his rickety old bicycle up and down the sidewalk. Most neighbors didn't speak to him, and he seemed to have little interest in speaking to anyone else. He was just a quirky neighborhood fixture who blended in with the brick houses and maple trees that took up residence on our lazy lane. His name was Rudy, but the neighbor kids called him "Rudy with the Cooties."

One sunny summer afternoon, I tried to befriend this bike-riding reptile as I walked out to the mailbox to send in our electric bill. I cheerfully greeted him as he rode by. He looked at me quizzically, but then began to pedal faster as he rode off down the street toward his house.

"Don't bother trying to talk to him," advised a neighbor, who was out watering her petunias. "He's weird and he won't answer back."

Being a social butterfly who is always up for a good challenge, I decided that one way or another, Rudy with the Cooties and I would become friends. And so every time I saw him, I smiled and waved. I complimented him on his bike-riding prowess or his snazzy dinosaur costume. Each time, I received the same response: a puzzled look and a speedy getaway. That was until one September afternoon.

The big yellow bus had just dropped off the children at the bus stop out front. About twenty minutes later, I heard a knock at my door. I opened it and was surprised to see Rudy standing in front of me, not in his signature Tyrannosaurus Rex tuxedo, but in tattered jeans and a soiled T-shirt. He was clutching a brown paper lunch sack in his left hand and staring down at his shoes.

"Why, hello, Rudy," I said joyfully.

His head still lowered, he held out the bag toward me and mumbled, "Hey, lady, would you like to buy some rocks?"

"Well, let me see what you've got there."

I took the stash of goods from his hand and opened it slowly. One by one I pulled out the small rocks—many laden with dirt—and raved about their uniqueness. I commented on their colors. I pointed out their various shapes. After a few minutes of shopping, I chose three stones and asked him how much they cost. "A nickel apiece," he replied, uttering only the second sentence I'd heard him speak in the nearly six months I'd known him. I walked across my living room and dug into my coin purse, retrieved a shiny quarter, and handed it to him. When he began to fret because he didn't have any change to give me, I smiled and quipped, "Oh, no! Keep the change. These three beauties are worth a quarter for sure." He took the silver coin from my hand, and still clutching his sack of stones, hopped back on his bike and dashed off.

Once or twice a week, this became our retail ritual. He'd knock. I'd answer. He'd show me his latest commodities. I would choose my three favorite stones and hand him a quarter. He would hop on his bike and dart away.

Then one day the knock on my door came from someone else. When I answered, a woman was standing in front of me. It was Rudy's mother. She struggled to find the right words, but relayed to me how grateful she was that I had shown kindness to her son.

"Most people round here think Rudy's strange and, well, I guess he is . . . a little. He doesn't have friends. No brothers or sisters. And I'm busy working two jobs so he's alone quite a lot. No dad neither. He left us long ago."

I invited her to come in, but she insisted that she needed to get ready for work. I assured her it was my pleasure to get to know her delightful son. She smiled and turned and walked quickly down the sidewalk, back toward her dingy home with the peeling yellow paint.

A few days later I was out on our apartment patio, pulling up faded marigolds and impatiens whose vibrancy had not survived the first frost of fall. As I pulled up the last marigold, I noticed that the corner where my husband had put a few landscaping stones was now bare dirt—the stones were gone. I had been purchasing my own rocks off of Rudy the entrepreneur!

As the years rolled by, we got to know this boy and his mama even more. We took him to our church's vacation Bible school. We invited him in for snacks. I reached out to his mom, stopping by to visit on her front porch when I would go for a walk. She even invited us to a birthday party she threw for her son's tenth birthday. Besides his grandparents, we were the only guests. She made us the most delicious fried chicken dinner and to-die-for chocolate cake with a layer of thick frosting that easily held up Rudy's ten candles. We brought him both a present and our presence. I'm not exactly sure which one he enjoyed more.

Today Rudy cheerfully helps customers at the parts desk of a local automotive store. Whenever he sees me, a huge smile flashes across his face, and I am reminded just how much of a blessing came from God prompting me to befriend him. He nudged me to see beyond the weird and find something wonderful instead.

God Sets the Lonely in Families

Reaching out to a lonely soul is a beautiful thing. I have been the one to reach out, but I have also been the lonely soul. Like as a high school student back in the 1980s.

"How did you know?" I inquired as I stared at the package I'd just opened. It was the fall of my junior year in high school. I had recently begun attending the little white church across the street–the one whose towering steeple seemed to keep watch over my sleepy, unassuming town. The woman who was married to the pastor of the church had begun to reach out to me. She invited me to play on the church softball team and also to attend the youth group that met every Sunday night. Although I wasn't sure about all of the church folk I had met thus far, something about her stood out. Her enthusiasm was contagious. Her loving personality was magnetic. And that day, she showered me with love as she gave me an impromptu gift of a Hallmark card and a teen devotional book. I had recently gotten a Bible, but I'd also wanted a particular popular devotional book. I remember it was called *If God Loves Me, Why Can't I Get My Locker Open?* I was elated when I unwrapped the gift and spied that book.

Miss Pat enfolded me into her family. I stopped by for snacks after school. She hired me to babysit her toddler and kindergartener. She asked about my school, my activities, my relationships—my life. Although I lived with an incredible single mom who gave me a wonderful life, the fact that my mom needed to work full-time meant I was often home alone. Knowing I could saunter over to Miss Pat's house to be around the hustle and bustle of a family helped to pass the time. And being around a woman who loved and served God helped to grow my newfound faith.

My relationship with Miss Pat—and my friendship with Rudy with the Cooties—showed me in a very tangible way the truth of Psalm 68:6, "God sets the lonely in families." Once upon a time, I was the lonely one looking for companionship. Now I can be the one with room at my table—or space on my sofa—for someone who is in need of such love and acceptance.

Albert Barnes (1798–1870), in his work *Notes on the Whole Bible*, wrote the following about Psalm 68:6:

> God is the friend of the orphan and the widow; and, in like manner, he is the friend of the cast out—the wandering—the homeless; he provides for them a home. The meaning is, that he is benevolent and kind, and that they who have no other friend may find a friend in God. At the same time it is true, however, that the family organization is to be traced to God. It is his original appointment; and all that there is in the family that contributes to the happiness of mankind—all that there is of comfort in the world that depends on the family organization—is to be traced to the goodness of God. Nothing more clearly marks the benignity and the wisdom of God than the arrangement by which people, instead of being solitary

wanderers on the face of the earth, with nothing to bind them in sympathy, in love, and in interest to each other, are grouped together in families.[3]

God certainly has the means to comfort the afflicted (and perhaps afflict the comfortable, who might see such reaching out as being *waaaaay* out of their comfort zone!), but he chooses to work through us and through our families. He draws others to himself through our voices, our food, our love, and our lives.

No More Lone Ranger Living

God's plan all along was that people would do life in community. To be connected with others. To share joys and concerns. To live out the great vertical fellowship with their Creator through the horizontal connections with their fellow humans. We see this concept through-out Scripture.

In Genesis 2:18 we read what God declared after creating Adam: "It is not good for the man to be alone." Aloneness wasn't good in God's eyes. So he created Eve to be Adam's counterpart, forming the very first marriage, and then with the birth of their children, the very first family.

Later, in Ecclesiastes 4:7–12, we read this observation by King Solomon:

> Again I saw something meaningless under the sun: There was a man all alone; he had neither son nor brother. There was no end to his toil, yet his eyes were not content with his wealth. "For whom am I toiling," he asked, "and why am I depriving myself of enjoyment?"

This too is meaningless—a miserable business! Two are better than one, because they have a good return for their labor: If either of them falls down, one can help the other up. But pity anyone who falls and has no one to help them up. Also, if two lie down together, they will keep warm. But how can one keep warm alone? Though one may be overpowered, two can defend themselves. A cord of three strands is not quickly broken.

And in the New Testament, Jesus himself modeled this principle when he sent out the disciples not as a solo act but in pairs to spread the good news of the kingdom (Luke 10:1).

God works in community. His plan is for people to be in relationship with each other. This is even more crucial when a member of humanity is dealing with loneliness, uncertainty, or rejection. Might those of us who have the means available to help lighten their loads and lift their spirits be ever on the lookout for such individuals, so we can carry out God's plan to set the lonely in families.

I know such a mission seems sentimental and spiritual. A good thing to do. The *right* thing to do. But often I am so busy living my life and dealing with my people that I don't pause to see who might be feeling alone or left out and who might need to be tenderly tucked into my family—if even for a shared peanut butter and jam sandwich or an evening meal of pizza, purchased with a super-saver coupon.

We might feel our life is boring and our possessions are plain. Yet there are many who would love to share our seemingly mundane lives, simply to feel that they fit in and that their presence is wanted.

Of course at times I am simply selfish. I don't want to interrupt my schedule or my family's routine. Or give up time doing something I would prefer to do. Or I don't want to spend any of my hard-earned money, wanting instead to purchase something I would rather have. It is then that the words of the eighteenth-century preacher John Wesley challenge me to rethink my priorities:

> Do you not know that God entrusted you with that money (all above what buys necessities for your families) to feed the hungry, to clothe the naked, to help the stranger, the widow, the fatherless; and, indeed, as far as it will go, to relieve the wants of all mankind? How can you, how dare you, defraud the Lord, by applying it to any other purpose?[4]

Let's get about the business of relieving the wants of human beings, sharing love with others—especially the lonely and unloved. Here are some ways we can do just that.

BE A BAROMETER OF FEELINGS.

A barometer is a scientific instrument used in meteorology to measure atmospheric pressure. We need to become a feelings barometer, measuring the emotional state of others and sensing the pressure that they are under. Rather than being caught up in our own lives, too busy to notice, we can instead be keenly aware of those around us who are left out, lonely, and hopeless. When we do encounter such a soul, we can begin to ask God how we might help them feel wanted and loved. It might be through just a small gesture, such as a kind word spoken. Or perhaps we could invite them into our homes or meet them at a coffee shop to allow them space and grace to share their lives.

OPEN DOORS.

Your front door. Your pantry door. Your refrigerator door. And ultimately, the door to your heart. When we live with an open-door policy, remembering that what we have comes from God himself, we will be more willing to share our time and possessions with others. So don't keep those doors closed. Kick them wide open.

SOLICIT YOUR FAMILY'S IDEAS AND GET THEIR HELP.

It is a wonderful thing when a child catches a vision early in life for reaching out to those who are lonely, marginalized, and vulnerable. So get your kids in on the act. Have them be on the lookout for someone who may be sad or lonely. Then sit down as a family and share your findings. Perhaps one of your children will know someone who needs a little pick-me-up. Brainstorm as a family what you might do to reach out to this person and share God's love. Could you invite them over or take them along with you to an athletic or extracurricular event? Send them a bouquet of flowers or drop off a platter of homemade goodies? Even a simple gesture will show them that you were thinking about them and that you care.

ASK FOR HELP.

Sometimes a good back door to someone's heart is to actually ask *them* to help *you*. Is your neighbor a master gardener and also a recent widow? Ask her if she might spare a little time to help you to prune your rosebushes or tend to your tomatoes that don't seem to be faring too well this season. Pour her a glass of homemade lemonade or an ice-cold root beer and ask her to sit and visit for a while. She is sure to welcome the human interaction and conversation, as well as appreciate the fact that you value her horticultural expertise.

We once knew a gentleman who had recently gone through a divorce and was very lonely. But he was also a very good handyman. My husband and I hired him for all the odd jobs around the house that we couldn't seem to get to. I always made sure to have something fresh-baked on the counter to share with him, and I would ask him to sit and chat for a while. What could've been a quick home repair visit often turned into an afternoon of listening to him talk about important things in his life or just talking about random nothings as we enjoyed each other's company.

SHARE BOTH THE GOODIES AND THE GOSPEL.

If the person you are reaching out to is a believer, the potential for Christian fellowship is great during the time you are together. If they don't know anything about church—or especially about the Lord and salvation—your time together can be an opportunity for you to share the good news of Jesus. Don't feel you need to come up with a three-point sermon and deliver it perfectly. Don't plan ahead for what you will say. Just be prayerful and mindful, working the message of the gospel into your conversation gently and naturally.

I once knew a woman who led many lonely people to the Lord right at her old kitchen farm table, as they shared her famous cinnamon buns and split a pot of coffee brewed in her old stove-top percolator. Our homes are a wonderful avenue for evangelism. When we stop stressing about our homes being perfect, we can focus on blessing others instead, naturally sharing the good news of the redemption story.

PLAN TO GIVE BUT BE PREPARED TO ALSO RECEIVE.

What has surprised me most about attempting to live a life of welcome—sharing God's love with others—has been the way I have been blessed in return. While I may have started out the encounter thinking I was doing a good deed or showing mercy and kindness to the other person, often I have been the one to receive great love, and great life lessons too. I have felt wanted and needed. I have known the delight of using my spiritual gifts of encouragement and hospitality. I have received genuine love and affection from those who don't often get to express it.

I'm reminded of one of my favorite lines from a movie I adore, *The Blind Side.* When Leigh Anne Touhy is out to lunch with her highfalutin friends, one of them—upon hearing that her wealthy white family has taken in a black homeless boy—says, "You're changing that boy's life."

Leigh Anne's response is epic.

"No. He's changing mine."

─────── The Who and the Why ───────

So who are the lonely and the unloved, and why should we seek them out? Jesus gives us a clue when he provides us with a guest list for our next dinner party:

> "When you give a luncheon or dinner, do not invite your friends, your brothers or sisters, your relatives, or your rich neighbors; if you do, they may invite you back and so you will be repaid. But when you give a banquet, invite the poor, the crippled, the lame, the blind, and you will be blessed. Although they cannot repay you, you will be repaid at the resurrection of the righteous." (Luke 14:12–14)

In other words, when you want to throw a party or have a delightful time, don't just include your peeps. Don't merely send out an e-vite to all those on your Facebook friends list. Think about those who may never get invited to a party. Those who are socially marginalized or physically or mentally disabled. Those whom society has forgotten or shunned. Those who cannot repay you. But fear not. You will be repaid, all right. And you will have the joy of knowing you are modeling Christ to a broken world.

In reality, we are not only ministering to people who society dismisses. We might think we are helping the homeless. We might suppose we are giving a second chance to a rough-and-tumble teenager. We might feel we are showing love to the outcast or an odd duck. But actually someone else is the recipient of our love in action. Again, listen to Jesus:

"When the Son of Man comes in his glory, and all the angels with him, he will sit on his glorious throne. All the nations will be gathered before him, and he will separate the people one from another as a shepherd separates the sheep from the goats. He will put the sheep on his right and the goats on his left.

"Then the King will say to those on his right, 'Come, you who are blessed by my Father; take your inheritance, the kingdom prepared for you since the creation of the world. For I was hungry and you gave me something to eat, I was thirsty and you gave me something to drink, I was a stranger and you invited me in, I needed clothes and you clothed me, I was sick and you looked after me, I was in prison and you came to visit me.'

"Then the righteous will answer him, 'Lord, when did we see you hungry and feed you, or thirsty and give you something to drink? When did we see you a stranger and invite you in, or needing clothes and clothe you? When did we see you sick or in prison and go to visit you?'

"The King will reply, 'Truly I tell you, whatever you did for one of the least of these brothers and sisters of mine, you did for me.'" (Matthew 25:31–40)

In the eyes of those society forgets, we see the presence of our Savior. When we do it for the "least of these," we do it for Christ.

When Your House Becomes Their Home

"Hey, boys. Remember. Before we eat, we pray," I reminded the eight teenagers who were crowded around my kitchen island, ready to dive into some of my famous cheesy corn chowder and biscuits and some crunchy coleslaw. It was a Thursday afternoon in early October. My son, who was a junior varsity football player, had invited several of his teammates for a meal before they faced our fiercest rival on the home field that evening. After we said grace, thanking God for our food and asking him to allow our game to be injury free, the boys dug in to their dinner.

Naturally their conversation centered around the Panthers—the team we were up against that night—and how we hoped to avenge last season's loss to them, our only loss that year. There was also talk of the upcoming homecoming dance and who was taking a date and who was going stag. Then the conversation turned to one of the boys at our table—a tall teen named "Big Bubba," or "Big" for short.

Big's parents had divorced when he was very young. As a result of the divorce settlement, the court directed Big to spend one week with his mother and the following week with his father, repeating this practice fifty-two weeks a year. Thankfully, both of his parents resided in the same small town so the distance between their homes was just a few miles. But this living arrangement meant that Big often lived out of a duffel bag and his school backpack. I had gotten to know Big's parents over the years. They were loving people who were trying to make the best of an unfortunate situation. This setup allowed both of them to spend equal time with their teenage son.

One of the boys eating dinner that night was not aware of this family arrangement and so he began to question Big about it. "Wait. Dude. You mean that you spend one week with your mom. And then the next week with your dad. And then one week with your mom. And the next week with your dad. Is that right?" Big looked up from his nearly finished plate of food and slowly nodded his head. His friend continued his line of questioning. "Then, man. When you think about 'home,' which house do you think of?"

Big looked up at the ceiling for a moment, as if trying to decide. Then he glanced around my kitchen and living room—where he'd spent many before-game dinners and after-game sleepovers, and impromptu video game pizza parties—and then he replied, "I don't know. Probably this one."

My heart hopped up and lodged in my throat. *When he thought about home, he thought of my house?* I quickly turned around and pretended to finish washing dishes so he wouldn't see the waterworks factory now setting up shop in my eyes, threatening to send my contact lenses floating away. I loved this boy as if he were my own. But it never occurred to me that he might feel the same way about me—and about our family.

Big is just one of many of "my boys." Up until four years ago, all of our children were homeschooled. I loved our homeschooling years. It fit very well with our schedule since my husband worked second shift at the factory. If the children had been in traditional school—whether public or private—they would have only been able to spend time with their father for a little over twenty-four hours each weekend. But when our youngest son, Spencer, entered the eighth grade, my husband was put on the day shift. And so we enrolled Spencer in the local public school.

Spencer (much like his mother) is a social animal. He collects friends like others collect vintage postage stamps. It didn't take him long to forge many close friendships at his new school. Pretty soon my kitchen island began filling up with teenage boys. And sometimes teenage girls. Many of them, like me, are children of divorce. A few of them have even lost their mothers to cancer or, in one case, suicide.

As we opened up our home—and our pantry and fridge—to these teens, I grew to love them as my own. At last count, seven of them had listed me in their phone contact section as "Mom" or "Mama Karen."

This delights my soul. I love the fact that they feel they can count on me and I love feeling like I am giving back—becoming the person that Miss Pat was to me.

When we share love with the lonely, the boomerang of blessing lands right back in our lap.

So how about it? Can you create one more space at your table this week? Can you send that card or buy those flowers, cheering up a weary soul? Will you choose to see beyond the weird to the wonderful? I've got a nifty rock collection that says doing so can change someone's world—and yours.

As we close out our time together in this chapter, let these words of St. Augustine be our prayer this week:

God of our life, there are days when the burdens we carry chafe our shoulders and weigh us down; when the road seems dreary and endless, the skies grey and threatening; when our lives have no music in them, and our hearts are lonely, and our souls have lost their courage. Flood the path with light, run our eyes to where the skies are full of promise; tune our hearts to brave music; give us the sense of comradeship with heroes and saints of every age; and so quicken our spirits that we may be able to encourage the souls of all who journey with us on the road of life, to your honor and glory.

Amen. And amen.

ON THE LOOKOUT FOR THE LONELY

We spend much of our time rushing—to work, home from school, off to the church meeting, around town to run errands. If we don't take time to intentionally look for the lonely, we may miss them. But they are there, perhaps wondering if anyone sees them at all. Here are some ways to watch for those who could use a little noticing, along with some actions to follow through in showing them love.

♥ **At restaurants.** Do you spy someone eating alone? Is there a couple next to you who appears to take a call that upsets them during their meal? How about a mom alone with her kids looking like she is frustrated and could use a break? Talk to your server and pay for their bill anonymously. Instruct the server not to tell them who paid if they ask. Instead have them tell them it was to show them that God sees and loves them. You may also keep notecards on hand in your purse for such times. Jot a note expressing your sentiments or sharing an appropriate verse. Have the server give it to the person when they deliver the news that someone picked up their tab. If paying another's bill isn't an option for you financially right now, rest assured that the notecard alone will mean a lot!

♥ **In your neighborhood.** Relocating can be difficult. In years gone by, neighborhoods and towns had an organized "Welcome Wagon" that greeted people when they moved into a new home, providing a map of the city, helpful phone numbers and information, and often homemade goodies. Perhaps God is calling you to be the Welcome Wagon in your area. If a new individual or family moves in, take them some baked goods and brochures about local attractions. You could even make up a sheet with the names and numbers of a local doctor, dentist, plumber, electrician, and lawn care service to help them to get connected and save them time trying to locate such services on their own.

♥ **On the sidelines, in the bleachers, or in the carpool line.** When you are at your child's activity, do you spy an unfamiliar face? Try not to fall into junior high mode, forming a clique with the parents you know well. If there is a parent you haven't met yet—or one who is new to the sport or extracurricular endeavor—don't be shy. Introduce yourself. Ask about her child. Sit with this new friend in order to make her feel welcome.

♥ **In church.** Church offers one of the best places to look out for the lonely. Is someone sitting alone? Sit nearby and chat a bit before the service. Is there a child in your Sunday school class or youth group who doesn't seem to connect with others there? Gently find a way to draw him in. Do you know of someone who is sick or disabled or sorrowing? Loneliness goes hand in hand with grief and suffering, so find ways to come alongside those who need extra support and encouragement.

♥ **Don't forget the elderly, shut-ins, disabled, newly divorced, or those who are caregivers.** These people long for human contact. Some long for a needed break. Make it a matter of prayer, asking God what you might do to encourage them. You could include the elderly, shuts-ins, or disabled in your normal family activities, taking them along to a concert, movie, or sports outing, or visiting them where they live. You could take the newly divorced parent's children shopping to buy them a gift for a holiday or their birthday. This will be especially helpful if the children are younger. Give respite to the caregiver by offering to stay with their loved one while they run errands or enjoy time away. It is sure to be a welcome stress reliever!

CHAPTER 8

The Cranky and Cantankerous

HOW TO LOVE THE HARD-TO-LOVE

Despite everything, I believe that people really are good at heart.

—ANNE FRANK

"But love your enemies, do good to them, and lend to them without expecting to get anything back. Then your reward will be great, and you will be children of the Most High, because he is kind to the ungrateful and wicked."

—LUKE 6:35

Children love stories. Whether it is a Walt Disney classic book or new release on the big screen, an old-fashioned fairy tale or a crazy impromptu bedtime story, kids love to listen to stories unfold.

As a child, I was no exception. I was especially drawn to plots in which a main character started out mean but experienced a change of heart through the love or kindness of someone else.

One of my favorites is the timeless *Beauty and the Beast*, a French fairy tale first published in 1756 and much later a popular Disney movie and Broadway show. In this story, a cruel prince who refuses to help an old hag is put under a spell and transformed into a hideous beast. The only way he can break the curse is if he experiences true love. Now, it is a tad bit difficult to get a woman to fall in love with you when you are a gruesome creature. The heroine of the story sees beyond his awful exterior, however, and eventually falls in love with the beast, who is then magically transformed back into his princely self. Happily-ever-after happens because Beauty saw beauty in the beast.

I still love a story about someone who goes from being cantankerous to kind as a result of being shown tenderness and love. I was blessed to see one such tale unfold in real life the year after I got married.

The Tale of Big Bad John

Other than being a writer and speaker, the job I've loved most in my life was being a substitute teacher for five years in the local public schools. While that vocation evokes images of chewing gum wads being placed on chairs, paper airplanes flying when your back is turned, and strategically placed "kick me!" signs, this was not my experience.

It may be because my husband was a youth pastor in the community and well-known by many of the students, but I never got an ounce of trouble from any of the students. While most of the substitute teachers on the roster asked not to be placed at the middle school, it was actually my favorite place to teach. Sure, the kids were squirrely, the girls were giggly, and the boys tried to act tough. But I chose to see a group of kids who were growing into their personalities in a sometimes tumultuous social setting. My heart went out to those adolescents, and I simply loved showing up for work.

One day, though, I thought my streak of trouble-free kids was about to be broken. That was the day the principal walked down to my room before first hour began. Surprised to see him at my door, I asked him how I could help. He replied, "I just wanted to let you know that today in third hour you will have a student named John _____. Just go ahead and send him down to the office before class starts."

I was puzzled by the request. The principal explained, "He is known as Big Bad John, and he has never successfully made it through even one hour with a substitute teacher. He will just disrupt the class, bully another student, and try to make you look stupid in front of the kids. I want to spare you any confrontation with him."

I knew exactly which student he was talking about. In his role as a youth pastor, my husband went once a week to both the middle school and high school for lunch period. Todd didn't choose to hang out with the kids from our church and youth group, though. Instead, he chose to hang out at the detention table with all of the students who had been placed on "house arrest" for bad behavior. This was much to the chagrin of some members of our church, who felt that he should be spending time with *their* children. But Todd believed that if Jesus were visiting a middle school lunchroom, the detention table was where he would sit.

At first some of the students teased him, wondering what this Jesus-dude wanted and why in the world he would ever sit with them. But Todd never gave up. Week after week he sat with these students—mostly boys—and got to know them. He'd greet them when we saw them out and about around town. He would introduce me to them like they were his friends. Slowly, he earned their respect. But not all of them. And certainly not John. Big Bad John didn't like *any* adults.

I'm sure other subs thought I needed my head examined, but I wanted a chance to reach this troublemaking teen and I certainly didn't want to give up before I even started. So I petitioned the principal. "Are you sure? May I just attempt to keep him in class and then send him to the office if he causes trouble? I'd really love to try, if you don't mind."

The administrator looked at me as if I had three heads. "Be my guest," he laughingly replied. "I'll expect him shortly after class begins."

Throughout the morning, I anticipated my time with this legendary student. I prayed that God would show me a way to get through to him. A way to treat him with kindness. And respect. To see beneath his tough exterior clear down to his potential. Then the class bell rang indicating that second period was finished. The students had five minutes to get to their next class. Just before the opening bell of third period rang, a towering and husky student appeared in the doorway. I just knew it was Big Bad John.

His appearance was somewhat disheveled, his long sandy blond hair looking as though it hadn't been washed in a week. His face was dotted with acne, his teeth crooked. He had on ripped jeans—in a time period way before they were fashionable—and a soiled light blue T-shirt. I could tell from the way the students stayed away from him that his odor was as unpleasant as his appearance and personality. I shot up a quick and final prayer to God and then greeted this formidable potential foe.

"Well, hello!" I confidently said. "You must be John."

A smirky smile materialized across his unwashed face. "Yep," he replied. "I suppose you've heard 'bout me. I'll bet the principal told you to send me right to the office 'cause ain't none of you substitute teachers able to handle me."

"Nope," I replied, just as quickly and confidently. "I heard you were going to be in my class and I also heard you are a great kid. Do you mind helping me pass out these papers?"

Now it was John's turn to look at me as if I were a three-headed creature.

I wasted no time but handed him a stack of papers on *Huckleberry Finn* that the students were to read for their English class homework that day. "And when you are through with that, would you please run down to the library to grab the projector for our movie? I'd really appreciate it."

Big Bad John wasn't sure what to do. He began to pass out the papers, although not doing it in a way I would like. Some he threw on the floor. Others he used to play a game of keep-away with a girl in class. I followed along behind him and corrected whatever he did, picking up the papers on the floor or gently taking one from his hand to give to a student. I thanked him when he was through, making no comment on his behavior. Then I reminded him I needed that movie projector. (Yes, I said "projector." Not DVD player or even VCR. I was very young when I was a substitute teacher. A mere babe in the woods!)

I handed him a hall pass and crossed my fingers. Sure enough, a few minutes later he returned to the room pushing the projector on a wheeled library cart. He told me the librarian gave him a hard time at first, not believing that he was there to pick it up. But when he showed her his hall pass, she relented. I asked him to take his seat and I began to show the movie to the class.

During the movie, John began to act in accordance with his nickname. He started to be disruptive, not just talking to his neighbors but taunting them. I walked over to his chair and squatted down next him. I then looked him in the eye and firmly but gently said, "Hey, look, John. I know that you have a reputation of never being able to make it through an hour with a substitute teacher. But I say today we show the principal a thing or two. I know you can cooperate. I know you are a good kid deep down inside there. I'd love for that good kid to come out today and for us to be friends. Are you willing to give it a try, just this once?"

"Who are you, lady? And who told you I was a good kid?"

I told him I was Todd's wife, the churchy guy who sat at the detention table once a week. He laughed as if to acknowledge that he knew who that Bible nerd was. But something in Big Bad John softened that day. Every few minutes he got restless and began to act up again. But I would shoot him a look or remind him of how many minutes were left in the class. He didn't have much longer to behave before we would prove the principal wrong.

Speaking of the principal, he popped his head into my class after about the first ten minutes, wondering why I had not sent John down to the office yet. I assured him that we were doing just fine. In fact, John was serving as my assistant that day. He gave me a puzzled look and shook his head. "Whatever you say," he quipped. I'm sure he reckoned that this novice sub would wake up and smell the cappuccino soon.

For the last fifteen minutes of class, John actually watched the movie without disrupting the session at all. Once the bell had rung, it was time for lunch. I marched straight down to the principal's office and told him that John had done just fine. The office was already buzzing with the news that this school bully had made it through an entire hour with a substitute teacher. And I was grateful to God that I didn't just take the easy way out but decided to choose to love the unlovable.

After that, whenever I had John in one of my classes, he behaved well. In fact, when he saw me outside of class at a basketball game or the grocery store, he made it a point to smile and wave and say, "Hi, lady."

I wonder just how many big bad people would have their icy cold hearts melted by a little dose of undeserved love.

Upside-Down Living and Loving

It's easy to love those who are lovable. It's a breeze to be kind to people you like. But to display the same behavior toward the outcast, the odd duck, the devilish, or the different is an altogether special assignment. Jesus not only taught it, he modeled it.

Throughout the New Testament, we see Jesus spending his time on earth with the not-so-popular people. He didn't just hang out with the social elite or the wealthy and influential. No. He touched the leper. He granted dignity to the prostitute. He welcomed the children and the tax collectors and the cheats and those society rejected. His last conversation at his crucifixion was with a thief who hung beside him, convicted and sentenced to death due to his unlawful behavior. But Jesus granted him entrance into paradise because of his remorse. Jesus modeled upside-down living and loving.

In addition to loving people who were socially marginalized, Jesus loved those who hated and despised him. Those who treated him terribly. He encouraged his followers to do the same, without excuse.

In Luke 6:27–36 we catch a glimpse of the Lord's seemingly backwards teaching:

"But to you who are listening I say: Love your enemies, do good to those who hate you, bless those who curse you, pray for those who mistreat you. If someone slaps you on one cheek, turn to them the other also. If someone takes your coat, do not withhold your shirt from them. Give to everyone who asks you, and if anyone takes what belongs to you, do not demand it back. Do to others as you would have them do to you.

"If you love those who love you, what credit is that to you? Even sinners love those who love them. And if you do good to those who are good to you, what credit is that to you? Even sinners do that. And if you lend to those from whom you expect repayment, what credit is that to you? Even sinners lend to sinners, expecting to be repaid in full. But love your enemies, do good to them, and lend to them without expecting to get anything back. Then your reward will be great, and you will be children of the Most High, because he is kind to the ungrateful and wicked. Be merciful, just as your Father is merciful."

When we do good to those who would seek to harm us or show love to those who mistreat or talk badly about us, we are modeling Jesus' behavior. He was merciful, just as God our Father is merciful. It is a countercultural idea to love the unloving. But it is God's plan for us.

In order to get to the place where we embrace such backwards living, we have to first learn to think of ourselves properly. Within the faces of the unlovely and hard-to-love, we must see ourselves. We must recognize that we too, at our very core, are unlovable as well. We are not perfect. We sin. We hate. We have cruel thoughts occasionally and sometimes display cruel actions. Because God showed us great mercy and kindness, overlooking our faults and forgiving our sins through his Son's shed blood on the cross, we in turn need to show mercy and kindness to those who seem hard to love. It begins with humility. In fact, later on in the book of Luke, Jesus addresses this concept:

> When he noticed how the guests picked the places of honor at the table, he told them this parable: "When someone invites you to a wedding feast, do not take the place of honor, for a person more distinguished than you may have been invited. If so, the host who invited both of you will come and say to you, 'Give this person your seat.' Then, humiliated, you will have to take the least important place. But when you are invited, take the lowest place, so that when your host comes, he will say to you, 'Friend, move up to a better place.' Then you will be honored in the presence of all the other guests. For all those who exalt themselves will be humbled, and those who humble themselves will be exalted." (Luke 14:7–11)

When we are operating from a posture of humility, it is easier to open our hearts to those who might seem difficult to love. It is then that we can put action to our thoughts and feet to our prayers. We can begin to seek out those who least expect to be noticed. To share a kind word. To meet a need. To touch a heart. Ultimately, to change a life.

- How to Hug a Porcupine and Squeeze a Skunk -

Do you know someone who is difficult to love? The nosy neighbor. The grouchy grocery store clerk. Your child's teacher who never cracks a smile. The hot-tempered boss. The church curmudgeon. Here are some things to keep in mind as you try to share the love with them.

PRAY. PRAY. AND THEN PRAY SOME MORE.

Any encounter with a difficult-to-love person must start off with prayer. Pray for them. Ask God to soften their heart to receive his love through you. Pray for yourself, asking God to show you the best approach for reaching out. Pray that he would allow you to hear any heart drops, spoken or unspoken. Perhaps just observing their behavior will give you clues into how you might touch their lives. And most of all, pray that you will not chicken out! Hugging porcupines and squeezing skunks is not for the faint of heart! You will be tempted to back out and visit your sweet grandmother instead for an easy good deed. Ask God to give you both creativity and boldness as you reach out to those who are challenging.

GO SLOW.

Don't make the mistake of going too quickly. Many challenging people are cautious in their relationships. They are not going to be your best friend right off the bat. Why, they may not even want to open the door when you knock! Pace yourself.

A number of years ago, we moved into a neighborhood next door to an elderly gentleman who was simply known as "The Man." He wasn't just grumpy, he was combative. He yelled at the neighborhood children playing innocently in the street. He chased dogs with a shovel, trying to take a swipe at them. Everyone from the mail carrier to the cable guy knew about the disposition of this belligerent gentleman. We instructed our kids to be kind to him, no matter how he acted. When he hollered at them as they rode their bikes down the street, they answered back respectfully, calling him "Sir." My husband and I consistently smiled and waved at him every time we passed. It took more than three months, but finally one day he raised his hand as if to wave back. No smile. No eye contact. But he did acknowledge our existence, which we chalked up as a major victory. He even grunted at me one Easter weekend when I baked banana bread and took it over to him. (He didn't chase me out of his yard since his wife answered the door with him that day. Boy, was I relieved to see her face!) Slow and steady wins the race to touch the heart of the cantankerous.

BE CURIOUS.

Don't write off those who are hard to love. Be curious. Investigate. There must be some reason why they behave the way they do. In the case of our neighbor, "The Man," we learned he was struggling with the early stages of Alzheimer's. Having been a military man and successful in business, he probably was terrified of his impending decline and loss of control.

Other people we have known who were prickly like

a porcupine and resisted our gestures of love had issues from their past. One mother had lost two sons in two different car accidents, blamed God, and wanted nothing to do with him. With her I had to be very careful not to talk about God in a way that seemed flippant or that trivialized her pain. I mostly just attempted to get to know her and be kind to her. Eventually, she came to the women's Bible study I was teaching at our church. Toward the end of the study, she opened up about her anger at God for letting both of her sons be killed. Often there is more to the story than meets the eye, so be prayerfully curious as you decide how best to reach out.

SERVE.

Sometimes the best strategy is to keep your mouth shut and your hands open. Look for ways to serve. Does that grouchy neighbor need his yard raked? Does he need you to pick up something at the grocery store the week that the roads are icy and he is home with a bad cold? Could the church curmudgeon's garage use a good cleaning out and your family happens to have Saturday morning free? Is there a group of people in your city who are considered "less than" by society? The homeless. Those in prison or in trouble. Remember them as well. Often, organizations designed to help others are short on volunteers.

With all of these folks, look for ways to serve rather than speak. Sometimes the best sermons are lives well lived. Remember the old saying, "Preach the gospel always. When necessary, use words."

KEEP SHOWING UP.

When your benevolent gestures are ignored or met with ungratefulness, it is tempting to throw in the towel. But keep showing up. Keep being the hands and feet of Jesus. Don't get discouraged if the person you are trying to love doesn't seem to notice at all. They do. Often they just do not want to show it. So keep showing up. Consistently. Lovingly. You will learn to read signals from others alerting you when to back off, but you can always keep showing up in prayer. Loving difficult people takes tenacity. Especially when they never show signs of thankfulness. Which leads us to our next point . . .

EXPECT NOTHING IN RETURN. ZERO. ZIP. NADA.

Don't expect to make the local paper when you give grace to the grumpy. Don't expect that the hard-to-love one will thank you or even acknowledge what you do. The only way to go about loving the difficult is to expect nothing in return. If we do good in order to gain accolades or to receive praise, or expect to convert someone and have a great redemptive story to tell, we will quickly give up. We love others out of obedience to God. Then we leave the results to him. When your expectation bar is lowered all the way down, you will not have to fear being disappointed by their lack of response. So expect nothing in return. Zero. And then finally . . .

GLANCE AT THEM, BUT FIX YOUR GAZE ON JESUS.

It is Christ himself you are serving. When you look at others, choose to see him. Remember that whatever you do for them, you are actually doing for the Lord. When we keep this perspective in mind, it will help us to keep on keeping on. Jesus is the ultimate object of our service, love, and affection. Choosing to see through others to him is crucial to maintaining our momentum.

So what about the people in your life today? Is there someone you find difficult to like—let alone love? Have you ever stopped to consider that this person (or maybe persons!) are on-purpose people in your life? God has placed them there for a reason. Is he calling you to reach beyond your four walls, breaking through your comfort zone, in order to show the love of Christ to someone who is either hard to love or socially marginalized? Remember, as you reach out to them you are honoring and serving the Lord.

Take some time in prayer today, asking God to show you whose heart needs softening by a kind gesture from you sent their way. Remember, "The King will reply, 'Truly I tell you, whatever you did for one of the least of these brothers and sisters of mine, you did for me'" (Matthew 25:40).

Father, when I encounter a person with a less-than-lovely disposition, may it not derail me from sharing your love with them. Help me see beyond their harsh or difficult exterior. May I love with no strings attached, expecting nothing in return. I want to do it as though I am doing it for you. In Jesus' name. Amen.

LOVING THE WEAK AND THE WICKED

As we make an effort to love the hard-to-love, we often will have to discern the difference between what I call "the weak" versus "the wicked." The weak are those whose bad behavior could have some understandable cause: mental illness, for example, or a personality disorder, past abuse, current difficult circumstances, and so on.

In contrast, the wicked are those who deliberately and continually pursue evil. When dealing with the wicked, we might be called to demonstrate moral muscle by standing up to their evil, which means exhibiting the "tough" side of love. This type of response might involve pointing out the bad behavior—as Jesus did with the religious leaders of his time—or setting boundaries in place so the evil cannot continue. For the "pleasers" among us, as well as those who have been victims of the evil, such confrontation may be difficult or nearly impossible. And for the tough among us, it may be hard to do this without seeming condemning or self-righteous. When done right, bold truth-telling can awaken respect and maybe bring self-knowledge in the other person.

Scripture directs that we are to be carefully and wisely compassionate to the weak (1 Thessalonians 5:14) but firmer with the hard-hearted and wicked (Proverbs 28:4), with more boundaries in place and consequences for breaking them clearly spelled out. Here are a few guidelines when it comes to loving the weak and confronting the wicked.

♥ First, you need to discern whether their poor behavior is caused by a weakness (mental illness, personality disorder, abuse in their past, current circumstances, or a one-time problem) or wickedness (an ongoing hard-hearted choice to live in the wrong way despite being confronted about their behavior in the past). Some individuals have true struggles and personality disorders. Others are operating out of a perverse desire for evil. Begin by asking God for wisdom in deciding which scenario you are dealing with. Proverbs 2:12–14 states, "Wisdom will save you from evil people, from those whose words are twisted. These men turn from the right way to walk down dark paths. They take pleasure in doing wrong, and they enjoy the twisted ways of evil" (NLT). If you are still unsure of what you are dealing with or how to cope, consult with your pastor, a counselor, or a godly friend who is wise and experienced in the area of relationships. Don't go it alone!

♥ If you decide you are dealing with a wicked individual, tread carefully or stay away altogether. Drawing boundaries may be necessary. Proverbs 22:5 suggests that we move far from those who are intent on practicing evil in their relationships:

"In the paths of the wicked are snares and pit-falls, but those who would preserve their life stay far from them." What does this look like? Perhaps having a policy of leaving a family gathering when your combative relative begins to belittle one of your children, as they are well-known for doing. Or politely but firmly ending a phone call with them when they begin to spew venom your way. Convey to them that you will not tolerate their bad behavior and that there will be consequences when they choose to act inappropriately.

♥ Make it clear you are leaving the premises, not the relationship. While it may be necessary to remove yourself—and your family members—physically from the evil person, be sure to assure them that you still care for them and long to have a relationship with them, if they will agree to treat you with love and respect. Be sure that you are treating them the same way in return.

♥ Decide to put some distance in your relationship, if needed. Sometimes you may need to take a break in your relationship with a difficult person for a while. You can still love them from afar—send them a note or text them a message, for example—and just choose not to be in the same room with them. But keep this in mind: the reason to add some distance is to improve the relationship, not necessarily to sever it.

♥ Be willing to forgive and grant a second chance. If the other person comes to you asking for forgiveness and vowing to change, prayerfully and carefully accept their apology, but be wise. Be gracious, granting them another chance, but also exercise caution. If you see some of the old familiar and improper behavior start to resurface, you may need to distance yourself again or even dissolve the relationship in order to protect yourself and your family and to help the person recognize the evil in their conduct.

SANDPAPER SPOUSES

As iron sharpens iron, so one person sharpens another.

—Proverbs 27:17

"This is NOT what I signed up for!" I cried out to God as I sat cross-legged on the bedroom floor of our first apartment, my eyes stinging with hot tears. Out in the living room sat my husband—bewildered, completely exasperated, unable to handle his wife's volatile emotions.

I was a brand new bride of just six weeks. Our thank-you notes for the wedding gifts hadn't even been sent! But already I had buyer's remorse. Or I guess more accurately, "bridal remorse." All I knew was that this "Happily Ever After" thing was not so happy after all.

The first few years of my marriage were rocky and rough. I had envisioned a relationship of marital bliss. Flowers. Candlelight dinners. Holding hands at the movies. Long strolls on the beach.

Then the wall of reality hit. Instead of the candlelight dinner, it was burnt roast. When he once again came home late from work, I wrongly interpreted that as him caring little about my culinary efforts. We didn't get to the hand-holding at the theater much because we couldn't make up our minds about which show to see. And I strolled on the beach, all right—all alone—just after I stormed away from my husband following yet another argument.

Although we possessed a mutual love for each other (really we did), our personalities and approach to life could not have been more different! In fact, we joke today that if we went on one of those online dating sites, instead of matching us up as perfect soul mates, the computer screen would blink a bright red message: "DO NOT DATE! TOTALLY INCOMPATIBLE!"

Often, my husband and I just plain rub each other the wrong way. Yep. We're different. We are what I call "sandpaper spouses" and our rough-around-the-edges relationship often finds us turning to God when we feel like turning away from each other.

When we encounter conflict, I am verbal and process my thoughts quickly, backing him into a corner. He prefers to pause and ponder before sorting his thoughts or sharing his feelings. This difference makes him view me as critical and combative. And I label him an avoider, accusing him of caring little about resolving conflict.

When making decisions, he is methodical and thorough, carefully weighing all options. I prefer to decide in a snap and forge ahead to the next thing. This difference causes me to label him as indecisive and tempts him to brand me knee-jerk and impulsive.

Having a spouse who faces life differently can often tempt us to attack each other. But what if we were to flip the situation and see things that rub us the wrong way as blessings . . . that enable our spiritual growth?

The Bible states that "iron sharpens iron." If your kitchen knife is dull, you sharpen it by grinding it against a rough stone, not by rubbing it on cushy cotton. In the same way, the rough patches in our personalities can help sharpen us in the areas of love, compassion, and patience—mostly patience!

And I know from experience that my less-than-perfect marriage has grown my prayer life immensely as I take my concerns to God during times of tumult.

My husband's slower-paced decision making causes me to pause and pray before I forge ahead and consider other options I might not have thought of initially. My verbal processing encourages my husband to talk through issues rather than stuff his feelings inside, where they might fester and explode later. And our different philosophies teach us patience and perspective.

Will you join me today in thanking God for sandpaper spouses? Rather than our differences driving us crazy, instead may they drive us all straight to our knees.

CHAPTER 9

Nearest and Dearest

HOW TO REALLY CARE FOR YOUR CLAN

Happiness is having a large, loving, caring,
close-knit family... in another city.
—GEORGE BURNS

Above all, love each other deeply, because
love covers over a multitude of sins.
—1 PETER 4:8

One sunny day in mid-January I was sitting at my in-laws' oak farm table, sipping coffee and nibbling on lavender shortbread, when I looked up to see my husband's mom handing me something she had been hiding underneath the table.

"But wait. What is this for? It's not my birthday. My birthday isn't until March," I protested as she scooted across the table a package wrapped in purple and tied with pink curly ribbon.

"I know," she replied cheerfully. "This is an unbirthday gift for you."

Excited, I unwrapped the box to find inside a gorgeous, snow-white, porcelain nativity set. Even now, over two decades later, its fragile pieces grace my china hutch every Christmas season. And when I spy this nostalgic piece of holiday décor, I secretly smile at my husband's family's practice of giving unbirthday presents.

Over the years, I have been the recipient of many unbirthday gifts from my mother-in-law and my sister-in-law. An antique milk bottle holder to hold the bottles I've collected from towns where my husband and I have lived. Decanters of sweet-smelling perfume. A new winter sweater. A pewter platter to serve appetizers for our family get-togethers. A hand-painted antique porcelain vase with cheery red strawberries on it that perfectly matches a set of candlesticks I once found at an estate sale. While it is wonderful to be remembered on your actual birthday, I think these out-of-the-ordinary trinkets presented on random days are the best. In fact, our own immediate family has also adopted the practice of giving these spontaneous surprises to each other, usually for no reason at all.

In order to practice this Ehman family tradition, I have done what my mother-in-law does. I set up what we call "Mom's General Store," a storage area in our basement that houses a few large plastic totes where I can stash the things I find until I am ready to deliver them for someone's unbirthday. To keep my stash well-stocked, I am constantly on the lookout for markdown bins, clearance aisles, and price reductions on end caps at department and grocery stores. When I come across something I think a member of my family would like, I tuck it away in the bin. Then whenever I feel they could use a little pick-me-up, I will retrieve the item, wrap it, and deliver it for their unbirthday. Not only do I enjoy this practice, but my children also have gotten into the spirit of it and sometimes do it for each other or for my husband and me. Celebrating unbirthdays is a simple practice that keeps us sharing the love all year long.

After all, all of this talk about sharing the love with others just wouldn't be complete if we didn't talk about daily loving those with whom we share a last name or a bloodline.

Loving our families can be tricky. These are the folks we hold most dear, but they can also be the people with whom we experience the greatest conflict. Family relationships have the potential to be strong and loving as well as strained and tense. And sometimes this happens all on the same day!

What can we learn about loving our own people? Time to take a trip back to the Bible to discover some answers.

All in the Family

The Scriptures are not full of perfect people. They are certainly not full of perfect families. Quite the opposite, in fact. In the very first family, Adam and Eve's son Cain was so jealous of his brother, Abel, that he murdered him.

Later on, Old Testament patriarch Jacob swindled Esau out of his birthright with the help of his mother Rebekah. Laban tricked his son-in-law Jacob into marrying Leah, then made Jacob work even longer to marry the woman he really loved, Rachel. Later Jacob became a dad many times over, but he especially favored his two sons by Rachel: Joseph and Benjamin. Joseph's brothers became insanely jealous when Jacob gave Joseph a colorful coat, so they sold Joseph into slavery. (Sheesh! Jacob appears to win the prize for most episodes of family dysfunction in the Old Testament.)

Old Testament royalty acted no better. When King Saul became jealous of David, Saul's son and heir, Jonathan, chose his friend David over his father. King David committed adultery with Bathsheba, with the consequence of losing their first child. Later his own son Absalom turned against him.

Face it. Where there's family, there is potential for conflict. But there is also potential for lasting bonds to help us weather even the stormiest of times. Look at a key moment during Jesus' crucifixion, a stormy moment if there ever was one. One of the last things Jesus did was to entrust his mother, Mary, to his disciple John, so that she could be cared for, and John lovingly complied by taking Mary into his home (John 19:26–27). In order to forge a family that sincerely loves and cares for each other daily, we need to follow Jesus' example of loving consideration. We also need to take to heart the principles spelled out in Scripture. (For a convicting summary of some of those principles, read the "One Another" passages listed on pages 52–56).

So often it seems easier to love those who don't see us first thing in the morning. We pray for patience with our boss. We ask for wisdom to deal with our child's teacher. We petition God to help us to be kind to a neighbor. But we take our families for granted.

The admonitions in the Bible about treating others well also apply to those who use the last drop of milk without telling us or who ruin our new white shirt by washing it with their new red sweatshirt. Yes, those who tick us off most are still people whom God calls us to love and serve and honor.

Do our family members witness us treating others with more respect than we show to them? Do we speak kindly to those outside our family while hurling harsh words at our own kin? I know this has often been the case with me.

On more than one occasion I have witnessed my children using not the loveliest of tones when speaking with each other. They have been snippy. And snappy. They have interrupted each other and been rude while trying to have a conversation. When I have corrected them, they have gently—or emphatically—pointed out to me that I often use that same approach when talking to their father.

Ouch.

My kids are right. With others I am polite. Always the people pleaser, I want to be liked. I don't want to lose friends. I don't want to offend someone and risk the chance that they might not like me. And so outside our home I verbally hold it together. But often with my own family I let down my guard and let harsh words fly. I don't control my temper and I don't temper my words. Shame on me. But I suspect I'm not alone.

— A Verse for When It's *You* Versus *Them* —

I love the Amplified version of the Bible. This particular translation uses an expanded format to explain what particular words meant in the original Hebrew and Greek languages. This amplifies the meaning, thus the name of the version.

In the Amplified Bible, Proverbs 15:1 reads:

> A soft *and* gentle *and* thoughtful answer
>   turns away wrath,
> But harsh *and* painful *and* careless
>   words stir up anger.

Let's break that verse down, phrase by phrase, to see if we can gain a little help for acquiring loving lips when we address our clans.

The first word we read is *soft*. Soft is the opposite of loud. It is also the opposite of harsh. It conjures up the fur of a kitten or the comfort of a down-filled blanket. Are our words soft when we interact with our family members? Or would they better be described as rough and scratchy or hard? When conversing with a spouse or sibling or child—yes, even with your grouchy uncle—let's make it a point to speak softly. (Unless your spouse is hard of hearing, like the husband of one of my friends. In his case she has to speak *loudly* and *clearly*—and not be grumpy when she has to repeat herself!)

Next we have *gentle*. This adjective means mild in temperament, considerate, kind, and tender. I would venture to guess that if you polled my family members, this is not always the word they would use to describe my interaction with them. My temperament isn't always mild. Sometimes it's a little spicy! I am not always considerate when I speak, often caring more about getting across my opinion than listening to what the other person is saying. But gentle, it is. We are commanded to speak gently rather than severely.

Then we come to *thoughtful*. Now there's a lofty goal! How often do we just rifle off a reaction to someone without putting any thought into what we are saying? But Scripture calls us to be thoughtful when we are speaking to someone, especially when we answer them. This means we stop and think. We pause and pray. We don't just bark out something mindlessly, but we give careful attention to what it is we are about to say, striving our best to make sure it is appropriate and helpful.

What will be the result of speaking softly and gently and thoughtfully? Scripture says that doing so turns away wrath. I sure have seen this to be true, especially when I react properly to someone's question. You know, even those annoying questions—as when a child asks you for the fifth time that hour something that you have already told them you don't know the answer to yet. Or your mother-in-law calls for the third time that week to ask for your casserole recipe that she keeps writing on an index card—and then misplacing. Such questions don't always elicit my best answer. But when I make an effort to really think through what I'm going to say and then say it in a tone that is soft and gentle, wrath is often deterred. If I don't, the interaction can escalate into a full-blown argument. All right, then.

Let's look at the last half of the verse: "But harsh *and* painful *and* careless words stir up anger." Obviously these three words are the exact antithesis of the three words used in the first half of the verse. *Soft* is the opposite of *harsh*. *Gentle* is certainly at the other end of the spectrum from *painful*. And if our words are *careless*, then they certainly are not *thoughtful*. This triple threat of words will stir the anger in our hearts, spilling it over into our homes. If we want to show love to the people with whom we converse the most, we would do well to memorize, and then implement, the directives in this verse. Oh sure, it won't be easy. I'll be the first one to tell you that! But I will also tell you that when I choose to follow this verse's advice, my family relationships are far less strained.

Sometimes, we just can't find any tender and kind-hearted words because we are so steaming mad. In that case it is often best to just walk away. To pick up the conversation later once our tempers have simmered down a bit. This way we are less likely to have regrets over cruel and cutting comments we might be tempted to make.

Being loving with our words is where it all begins. But there are so many things we can do besides speaking kindly to our relatives that will share God's love with them and strengthen our relationships.

----------- **Family Matters** -----------

Here are some items to consider to help you not only show love to each other in your home but also foster a sense of family identity among your kin.

IT'S AN EHMAN (OR A _____) THING.

I love our family's little inside jokes, sayings, and preferences. For example, we holler, "Perch!" when someone is mad because they are losing during a family board game; it signifies that they are now up on their perch, pouting. Or my near-daily warning to my children, "Be sure your sins will find you out!" meant to help them remember to honor God and follow his ways. "You are the sum of your choices!" is another. Brie cheese melted with apricot jam on top and served with club crackers while playing cards. Yep. That's an Ehman thing, for sure! When we watch a movie together we eat massive mountains of butter-ranch popcorn made by our youngest son. For us, all of these things spell family and signify home.

Does your family have their own particular sayings and habits? Do you have any well-loved snacks or recipes that mark your family as unique? If not, consider acquiring some. The little sayings will just come out naturally. Or perhaps try passing on some you remember your own parents uttering. (Grandma Ehman was famous for the "sum of your choices" one!) And for the recipes and traditions, gather your clan around and ask them what they enjoy doing together. What snacks and meals do they enjoy and just can't live without? Frequency in traditions helps to solidify them in your family memories as something that spells love. Serve the snacks often. Play those board games. Take those hikes. Participate in the hobbies your family loves. Repetition will help those things become part of the DNA of your family memories.

PRACTICE ACTIVE LISTENING.

Listening is an art. And—just as in the only art class I took in middle school—I stink at it! Usually when someone else is talking, I am already thinking about what I want to say. Or my mind wanders. I wonder where she got her earrings. Or I'm trying to remember if I pulled the roast out of the freezer to thaw it yet. Or I'm thinking about what I need to pick up at the grocery store that afternoon. Listening is not my strength, but I'm working at it. My desire is not just to hear the words spoken but to hear the unspoken heart words as well.

One thing I have found helpful is to parrot back to my family the words they have said, making sure I have understood correctly. Sometimes I need to tell my husband or kids that if I can finish what I'm doing, I'll be able to listen more intently. This communicates to them that what they have to say is important to me. It also gives me a chance to be present with them because I've been able to get to a stopping point in my task. This is especially important with family members because often we try to multitask when they are talking. We may be reading the mail or making out the grocery list and only listening halfheartedly. Practice active listening with your family members this week.

EAT TOGETHER.

Wow. That felt weird to type. If it were decades ago, it would've seemed like a silly thing to encourage family members to eat together. Supper was always on the table at 5:30 p.m. and the family gathered round to enjoy Mom's cooking and share about their day. But oh, what a difference a few years—and many screens—make! Now our schedules are so packed that we rarely have time to enjoy family dinner. Or if we do happen to all be in the home at the same time and seated around the table, screens are vying for our attention. A couple practices can help us in this area.

First, as often as your family is able to pull it off, cultivate the habit of eating together. It might mean you have to adjust dinnertime. It might mean you have to say no to some outside commitments. It might mean you pick certain nights of the week where everyone is required to be present at the table. But make eating together a priority. And don't let all of the weight fall on Mom's shoulders to prepare the meal. Have your husband and kids pitch in and help with the preparation and the cleanup. If everyone eats, then perhaps everyone should have a responsibility in getting the meatloaf in the oven and the mashed potatoes in the bowl, as well as loading the dishwasher. In fact, cooking or cleaning up together can be wonderful times to share about what is happening in each other's worlds.

When you are eating, shut off the screens. People don't need to be texting or watching hilarious videos on YouTube (unless, of course, they want to share something with the family that they found particularly funny). Stare at each other's faces rather than Facebook walls. Talk rather than Tweet. Listen rather than "Like" photos on Instagram. When the family gathers in and tunes out distractions, real family fellowship can take place.

PLAY "ONE THING."

You may want to adopt this practice we have in our family. Sometimes we will gather in the living room for an informal time. Then we take turns going around the room, mentioning "one thing" we appreciate about each other member of the family.

Mom might tell a child how much she appreciates the effort that the child has been putting forth in a difficult class at school. A sibling might say to his brother or sister how he appreciates being able to borrow a prized possession or play with a favorite toy. Or he might point out how that person always pulls for the underdog or includes the lonely. A wife might thank her husband for the way he prays for his family every day. Playing "One Thing" helps get the conversation going as your family verbally praises each other for the character qualities they see.

SEND GROUP TEXTS.

Even though they have a tendency to blow up my phone, I love our family group texts. (My phone is beeping and buzzing with one now as I type!) We send encouragement. And goofy pictures we find. Maybe a crazy video or a link to an upcoming local event that we might enjoy going to as a family. We check in to see how each other's days are going and to say we are praying for one another.

Group texts are instant love messages sent through cyberspace. Start your own thread today! A blown-up phone is a beautiful thing.

PRAY. AND LET THEM KNOW YOU ARE PRAYING.

Let me ask you something. If you aren't praying for the members of your family, who is? Having a plan for praying for your family members is crucial. Attack this noble task in the way that makes sense to you. Perhaps you will want to get a small spiral notebook, give each person a page or section, and jot down the requests you have for them. Other people like to do this in a "notes" application on their phone. There are even some apps out there designed specifically for this purpose. "Echo," for instance, is simple and easy to navigate, and it will send a reminder to you at a set time to pray for a person. You can also do the same thing by simply using the alarm feature on your cell phone, setting a daily time for each member of your family.

Or perhaps you can do what I do: make yourself some prayer prompts. Whenever I wipe down a counter, which can be several times a day in my kitchen, I pray that God will convict my family members—and me—of any sin and that we would desire confession and forgiveness, wiping the slate clean. Whenever I brush my teeth, I pray for a few extended family members who are not believers—yet. When I am waiting for the hot water to come on in the shower, I pray for a cousin who is walking through a dark time in life right now. When I leave my small town to drive into the big city, I pray for my parents. Of course

I try to have a formal time of regular prayer daily, right after I read my Bible. But these prayer prompts help me to pray throughout the day as well.

Now, don't stop once you have uttered "Amen." Let your family members know you are praying for them. Send them a text message. Send a private message on Facebook. Or tell them face-to-face when you see them what you have prayed that day. It is such a huge encouragement to know that our family members are lifting us up in prayer.

ADOPT THE PRACTICE OF UNBIRTHDAYS.

Unbirthdays don't have to be just an Ehman thing! Pick up this practice in your own family. Choose one family member this week and purchase a small token of remembrance for them. Maybe it is something they have been longing for. Or perhaps it is just their favorite soft drink and snack that you are going to leave out on the desk in their bedroom. Send flowers or chocolate-covered strawberries to their workplace. Pick up a gift card to their favorite restaurant and tuck it inside a card, with a note telling them how much you mean to them. Unbirthday gifts, whether small or substantial, are fantastic ways to show love.

Somehow Forge a Family

I was raised in a single-parent family—a child of divorce when most people in my era and area still had intact families. I often felt sorry for myself. I wished I had two parents at home rather than just one. I grew tired of packing up and going to my father's apartment every other weekend. The only extended family I ever interacted with were my mother's mom and stepdad and her one sister and her family who had the only cousins I knew of. I often grew jealous of friends who had big families who spent lots of time together. When they would talk about their aunts and uncles and cousins, I wondered how many more of mine existed out there somewhere. My father had lost touch with his siblings and all of their children. I grew to believe that my extended family would just become one huge mystery in my life—a question mark that would not go away.

But as an adult, I was able to connect with family I never knew as a child. While on a trip to Florida as a newlywed, I stopped with my husband at the last town I ever heard that my biological grandfather lived in. In the phone book, I found his name, and I was able to meet with him. We exchanged letters until he died over a decade later. The advent of Facebook allowed me to connect with cousins on my mother's side. My father rekindled his relationship with his remaining living siblings, and so I was able to meet my ninety-four-year-old aunt whom I had not seen since I was about seven years old.

Seeing God connect these dots has been such a blessing in my life. Unearthing information about my relatives also alerted me to the fact that some died very tragic and sad deaths. Another one is in jail. I also learned that one cousin has an indoor potbellied pig for a pet. (Well, at least that is unique!) But these folks are my family. My blood. My heritage. Embracing my less-than-perfect family has been a picture of how God embraces me.

As a mom, I have also stopped trying to compare my small, immediate family to others who seem to have it all together. I spent far too many years being jealous of moms who kept impeccable homes and maintained amazing family traditions. (I know I may have caused the same jealousy in you. If so, I apologize. I want to share with you what we find works for us, but believe me, my family is far from perfect!) I have stopped wishing my children were quiet and mild-mannered, sitting still and causing little turbulence. I wholeheartedly embrace their personalities now. Two of them are adventurous and rambunctious. Argumentative and high-spirited. The other one is meticulous and methodical, prone to worry, contemplative. All three are loud. Shoot. Our entire family is loud. Everyone was just home for Thanksgiving last week and I could hardly hear myself think. But you know what? I loved every moment of it. Even when we were fighting over who was cheating in a rousing game of Balderdash and who ate the last of the brie!

So somehow, forge a family. Take all the irregular people that bear your name and share your heritage. God will place them together in the most beautiful of ways, forming a montage of magnificence. Every family is unique—with their own personalities, traditions and sayings, and favorite foods and activities. We should not all be exact replicas of one another. As we display love within the uniqueness of our family, we show the world how God draws us near, welcoming who we are.

So share the love in your family. Whether quiet or loud, messy or neat. Whether you dig into take-out burgers or dine on homemade pot roast. Whether you ski, sail, shop, snack, or swim together. Whether you have a family dog named Fido or a big ol' potbellied pig. Celebrate your nearest and dearest not just on their birthday or unbirthday but every day!

Father, thank you for my family members. All of them. For the ones with whom I find it easy to get along. And for the ones who get under my skin at times. I want to display love and respect to my relatives as much as I do to my friends and even strangers. Grant me patience, gentleness, love, and respect as I interact with them each day. In Jesus' name. Amen.

RELATIVELY SPEAKING

Presenting a family member with a token trinket is a great way to show love, but sometimes what is needed more is the gift of our words. Here are some ways to use your words—whether they are spoken, handwritten, texted, or posted—to show love to one of your clan.

♥ **Stick 'em up.** Once they are asleep, place a sticky note where they are sure to spot it first thing in the morning that says, "Just in case you were wondering, I'm glad you're my _____" (fill in the blank with *son*, *daughter*, or *husband*).

♥ **Mess up a mirror.** Grab a tube of lipstick or a wax pencil and scrawl out a message of encouragement on an important day for them. Perhaps your husband has a performance review at work or your child has an exam or audition later that day. Finish the statement with "I am praying for you." Then set an alarm on your phone so you remember to pray.

♥ **Type out a text.** Grab your phone and type out a text to a family member—whether near or far away—telling them you are thinking of them and hoping they are having a great day. Be sure to use lots of emojis! This is a simple way to show love that takes less than a minute from your day but might just make theirs.

♥ **Pack their lunch with love and lyrics.** If someone in your family carries a lunch to school or work, tuck in a little note with some song lyrics to brighten their day. Doodle on it a bit, adding musical notes, hearts, or smiley faces. Some ideas are: "You are the sunshine of my life" or "We are family. Get up everybody and sing!" for one of your kids or "I can't help falling in love with you," "I think I love you," or "Love will keep us together" for your spouse. You can even write it on the side of their banana with a ball point pen. So fun!

♥ **Resurrect the lost art of letter writing.** Pull out a pen and write a short letter to a family member expressing your love and appreciation for them. Including a fond or funny memory will especially make them smile. People love discovering handwritten, old-fashioned sentiments in their mailbox. Or, if they live with you, place it on their pillow along with a little treat of candy, nuts, or trail mix for them to find when they turn in for the night.

♥ **Prepare a post.** Hop on their Facebook page and craft a post that reads "The Top 10 Things I Appreciate about You." Think of ten characteristics and skills you love about your family member. Are they unselfish, always thinking of others first? Do they bake a mean banana bread or grill the best marinated chicken ever? Are they always quick with a crazy joke to brighten your day or to offer godly wisdom when you ask? Come up with ten things you most appreciate about them. Then don't keep it to yourself. Tell them—and all who will spy it on Facebook.

WHY I BUY
ORANGE MARMALADE

Do nothing from selfish ambition or conceit, but in humility count others more significant than yourselves. Let each of you look not only to his own interests, but also to the interests of others.

—Philippians 2:3–4 (ESV)

The sound of clanking silverware and clinking dishes wafted through the air as my husband and I sat across from each other in a retro-styled diner looking over the breakfast menu. We'd been meaning for weeks to spend some time alone, or maybe even go on a real date. So we set our alarms for still-dark o'clock and drove a half hour to the quaint eatery.

I'm not a big breakfast eater, so a steaming cup of coffee with fruit and nut oatmeal was enough for me. My husband, however, loves breakfast. So he ordered one of the diner's famous combo plates that included eggs, sausage, and a few pieces of whole grain toast.

He slathered some sweet cream butter on the toast. Then he began to dig through the gingham-lined basket on the table like a child digging through a toy box for a favorite plaything.

I had to know, so I asked: "What are you searching for?"

"Orange marmalade," he replied.

"What? Isn't grape jelly or strawberry jam good enough? You can't seem to get enough of my home-made strawberry jam," I teased.

"But orange marmalade is my favorite," he answered. "Loved it ever since I was a kid."

Wow. There I sat across from my college sweetheart-turned-husband whom I've known over a quarter century, and I never knew this simple fact—he loves orange marmalade.

Often in marriage—especially if there are children in the picture—we spend so much time just getting life done. Keeping up the house. Making appointments. Tending to the yard work. Shuttling children. Paying bills. And we stop noticing the little things about our spouses—the stuff we used to notice all the time when we were dating.

In college, I listened and took good notes on what my then-boyfriend enjoyed. I knew he was a lover of butter pecan ice cream, so sometimes I would pick up a hand-packed pint from the local ice cream parlor and deliver it to him when he was studying in the college library.

Back then it seemed easy to put him first, to always be on the lookout for his interests and likes. Selfishness on my part didn't really exist in our relationship. I was head over heels in love with this guy and intent on noticing his preferences and pleasing him.

Sadly, as the days and months of marriage turn into years and decades, it's easy for noticing to decrease and selfishness to creep in. Instead of longing to please our spouses, even in the little things, we often look to get our own way. Philippians 2:3–4 seems to be the perfect scriptural prescription for this dilemma. We are encouraged to look not just to our own interests, but also in humility look to the interests of others. There are so many ways to apply this verse in marriage!

It may mean spending a weekend doing activities your spouse prefers. In my case, that would mean attending a jazz festival on a Saturday with my trumpet-playing husband, rather than hunting for antiques at a large indoor market, which bores him to death.

Sometimes it might be a more important matter, and other times it could be a seemingly trivial thing. Again, in all things means not only looking to your own interests, but in humility looking to the interests of your spouse.

In a culture of selfies and selfishness, let's purpose to take notice of our spouse's interests and show him love in even the smallest of ways. For me, that means I'm now surfing the Internet for a winning orange marmalade recipe. Well, that and buying a few jars of the store-bought variety for backup!

CHAPTER 10

Scatter Kindness

OTHER-CENTERED LIVING IN A SELF-CENTERED WORLD

It's not what you gather, but what you scatter, that tells you what kind of life you have lived.

—HELEN WALTON

Command them to do good, to be rich in good deeds, and to be generous and willing to share.

—1 TIMOTHY 6:18

My kitchen contains some of my favorite things. My big red Dutch oven that holds a hearty beef stew or a simmering batch of chicken noodle soup. An antique pewter platter that came from my sister-in-law. A lovely watercolor painting of a bowl of fruit, purchased at an estate sale. And my aqua KitchenAid mixer. Because, well, I like to bake and I simply love the color aqua! But perhaps the object I adore most is a lettered sign my mother-in-law gave me for an unbirthday gift just after I married her son. Made from rustic barn wood, it is painted navy blue and has stenciled on it the simple phrase "Scatter Kindness."

I purposefully hung this inspiring inscription above the kitchen door that leads to the garage so I'm sure to see it every time I head out. Scattering kindness has become somewhat of a life mission for me, and I hope it is something my children catch a vision for as well. Every time I exit my home, I am entering a world filled with turmoil, sadness, and despair. Of course there are pockets of happiness and love too. On many days, though, it feels like the sadness overshadows the joy. It doesn't take much looking around to find a soul who is in need of a little encouragement or a healthy dose of hope.

I was once told that there are two types of people in the world: those who enter a room full of people and narcissistically announce, "Here I am!" and those who walk into a room, seek out someone, and lovingly declare, "There you are!" I want to be the second type of person. I want to make sure that life is about others and not just myself. And someday, when I am long gone, I hope those who knew me will remember me as someone who sought others out to encourage them, rather than sought only to make myself known. How about you?

Your One-Sentence Eulogy

The Bible tells detailed stories of the titans of the faith: Abraham, Joseph, Daniel, and Mary, to name a few. But sometimes it gives us an intriguing glimpse of some lesser-known characters, sketching their story in a sentence or two. One such character is the New Testament woman Tabitha.

We meet Tabitha in Acts, which is the story of the birth of the Christian church as recorded by a doctor named Luke. Of course, Acts introduces us to the founders of the church, including Peter and Paul. But tucked away in its pages we also find a portrait of a woman who demonstrated how to live alert and scatter kindness. I love her one-sentence description: "In Joppa there was a disciple named Tabitha (in Greek her name is Dorcas); *she was always doing good and helping the poor*" (Acts 9:36, emphasis added).

What a beautiful and unusual introduction! While most personal descriptions mention relationships ("a wonderful wife and mother") or career accomplishments ("a dedicated teacher"), this woman was known for continually looking for ways to show love to others. Concerned about the poor, she actively worked to make their lives better. In fact, her actions so radiated Christ's love that the author of Acts recorded these words for us to read two thousand years later in our Bibles.

One reason we know about Tabitha today is because she died, and Peter raised her from the dead. But as glorious as her resurrection was, her character is what impresses me. *"She was always doing good and helping the poor."* Oh, how this one sentence shakes my soul and stirs my heart. If someone were going to record a one-sentence eulogy about me, what would they say? How would they describe you? Would they observe about us—like Tabitha—that we were "always doing good"? Were we on the lookout for those who had a much harder row to hoe, or were we more concerned about our own safety and comfort, giving little thought to others?

While sometimes we may think our life is boring, could we see such humble and common circumstances as an opportunity to use our ordinary lives for God's extraordinary purposes, just as Tabitha did? I love this passage from Timothy that encourages us to ponder this very notion:

> In a large house there are articles not only of gold and silver, but also of wood and clay; some are for special purposes and some for common use. Those who cleanse themselves from the latter will be instruments for special purposes, made holy, useful to the Master and prepared to do any good work. (2 Timothy 2:20–21)

Oh, how the last part of that passage encourages me: "useful to the Master and prepared to do any good work"! We are useful to the Master, even though we may appear to be common. He has good works planned in advance for us to do. We just need to have an open heart, and a listening ear, as we seek to be available to do good to others.

Years from now, how do you want people to remember you? Take a little time today to think about what actions of yours speak the loudest. What will be your one-sentence eulogy?

God's Whole Point of Kindness

When our son Spencer was very small, he simply refused to wear socks and shoes. He found them rather confining and would much rather roam about with his little piggies set free. And so most often you would find him barefoot. Now most of the time this did not pose a problem, since he was happily playing in the house. But when summer came, a battle ensued. I insisted that he wear shoes when he went outdoors. But he simply loved running shoeless through the grass. As a result, many times I saw him in our backyard pulling off his shoes to run free.

One day when I saw him removing his shoes, I went outside to correct him. He refused. I tried to reason with him, telling him it was a safety issue. Because we lived out in the country where the county fairgrounds once stood, we never knew when we were going to find a stray piece of glass or a nail, and I didn't want him to get injured. At that point his four-year-old power of reasoning kicked in. In his protest he declared, "But *Moooooooom*! Barefoot is God's whole point of summer!"

I chuckled out loud when I saw the determined look on his face. He was trying his very best to convince me that even God thought it was a good idea for him to run around with no shoes on. After all, the very reason God invented summers was for young children to be able to freely frolic about, squishing the green grass between their toes.

When I think about the concept of scattering kind-ness and sharing love, I have to stop and wonder—what is

God's whole point in all of it? Why should we strive to be thoughtful, generous, and kind people? Is it so we will be well thought of? Is it so others will be cheered up? Is it to light a candle in the darkness? Is it to do our fair share of "good works" in order to earn our way to heaven?

Many religions are based on a good works mentality—if we do enough kind deeds for others, God will deem us good enough and let us into heaven. Christianity is just the opposite. It says we will never be good enough. Ever. In fact, we are so bad that we deserve to spend eternity separated from God forever in hell. However, Jesus—who is God's perfect Son—laid down his life for us, taking our punishment instead. By doing this he purchased our way to heaven and saved us from eternal punishment.

No, we are not saved by our good works. But we are saved in order *to do* good works. Ephesians 2:10 even goes so far as to assert that God planned since creation for us to do kind deeds: "For we are God's handiwork, created in Christ Jesus to do good works, which God prepared in advance for us to do." We can think about it this way: good works aren't our ticket to heaven. They are our marching orders here on earth.

So just what is God's whole point of us being kind—especially to those who might be different from us or even difficult to love? I believe it is this: because our kindness can be a conduit to help others to discover God's grace and accept his salvation. That is it. Which brings us full circle to what I learned from my mentor Miss Pat back when I was a teenager: There are only two reasons that we are here on earth. One is to have a relationship with God, thereby making it to heaven. And the second reason is to take other people with us.

But the people-loving business is a hard one. People can be prickly. And harsh. Even rude and obnoxious. Or they can be unfriendly and aloof. They might be shy and reserved and seem standoffish, making it difficult for you to reach out to them. Often it is easier to judge others than to love them.

I certainly have struggled with being judgmental. It is easy to pick apart the personalities and behavior of others when they don't approach life as I do or they make decisions that I would never make.

Judgment is rife in our culture—especially online. Just scroll through the home feed of Facebook or peruse the tweets on Twitter. Opinions and critical comments fly. It takes a little more looking to unearth kindness and respect. And often we forget—when we are judging others—that we ourselves are not perfect. We sometimes even do some of the same things for which we judge others!

However, *judgment does not win others over. Kindness does.*

In Romans 2:1–4 we read these words:

You, therefore, have no excuse, you who pass judgment on someone else, for at whatever point you judge another, you are condemning yourself, because you who pass judgment do the same things. Now we know that God's judgment against those who do such things is based on truth. So when you, a mere human being, pass judgment on them and yet do the same things, do you think you will escape God's judgment? Or do you show contempt for the riches of his kindness, forbearance, and patience, not realizing that *God's kindness is intended to lead you to repentance*? (emphasis added)

What an insightful passage! In it we catch a glimpse of God's whole point of kindness—both his kindness *and* ours. And we see the ill effects of judgment. It leads us nowhere and actually makes us hypocrites!

When and How to Judge

Christians don't always have the greatest of reputations. In fact, we're often associated with being judgmental. We are known more for what we stand against than for kindness, forbearance, and patience. How this fact saddens my soul.

But many are quick to point out that in certain places in the Bible, we are actually told *to* judge others. Yet Jesus himself said—in perhaps one of the most quoted verses of Scripture ever—"Judge not, that ye be not judged" (Matthew 7:1 KJV). What is going on here?

I believe our perspective on judgment is such a mess today because we don't realize that there are three types of judgment in the Bible. In fact, the original Greek uses three different *words* for judgment. Two types of judging we are encouraged to do, but the third is forbidden. The confusion comes because those three Greek words were all translated into English as the same word *judge*. Let me explain.

When Jesus told us in Matthew 7 that we are not to judge, the original Greek word is *krino*. It means to form an opinion of, and then to pronounce a sentence or condemn, much like a judge who hears a case, then finds the accused guilty, pronounces a judgment, and condemns them to time in prison. This is the type of judgment we are *not* supposed to do. We are not supposed to form our strong opinions and then condemn others, pronouncing them unfit for company. But sadly this is often what we see today. Too many Christians are quick to leap to opinions and then pronounce a "jail" sentence on others with whom they disagree.

Elsewhere in Scripture, it appears we *are* to judge. See, for instance, 1 Corinthians 2:15: "The person with the Spirit makes judgments about all things." It is important to note that the original word in this passage is *anakrino*, which means "to examine, question, investigate, and discern." No mention in this definition of pronouncing a sentence or condemning someone.

Finally, to make things really confusing, there is a third word that was translated *judge* in most of our English Bibles. This word is *diakrino*. This is the term used in 1 Corinthians 6:5: "Is it possible that there is nobody among you wise enough to judge a dispute between believers?" This word means "to discriminate or arbitrate," like a judge who decides who is telling the truth or one who settles a dispute between two people.

In short, it is fine for us to have processes in place that will arbitrate disputes. It is fine for us to evaluate, question, investigate, and discern so we can make informed decisions. But it is *never* okay for us to condemn someone else.

When we put judgment in its proper place, knowing that God is the ultimate and final judge ("He rules the world in righteousness and judges the peoples with equity," Psalm 9:8), we can focus more on the last sentence in the passage from Romans 2: *"God's kindness is intended to lead you to repentance."* God's kindness—not his condemnation—is what wins others to himself, and our kindness, as we behave as he would, can win others over too.

What Kindness Looks Like

What kindness looks like in life is this: I can spend time with others who are not Christians. I can be friends with someone who is not following God. While I should be careful to evaluate the influence they might have on me and act accordingly, I should not shy away from the influence my kindness might have on them developing a walk with Jesus. And I should be on the lookout for ways to reach out to them, reflecting God's love.

I have become friends with a woman who is an atheist. Yep. You read that right. I am a Bible teacher, but one of my friends denies that God even exists and thinks the Bible is a frivolous work of fiction. We became friends a few years ago when both our kids joined the same sports team.

Over these last few years, I have sat beside her in the bleachers, cheering our boys on. When we held a team potluck, and she made a delicious dish to pass, I asked her for the recipe. Sometimes we go out for lunch or estate sale shopping, looking for antique bargains. When one of her relatives passed away, my husband and I sent flowers to her house, along with a handwritten card telling her how sorry we were for her loss.

In my friendship with this woman, I try to show her with my actions a reflection of Christ. At first, she was a bit combative and wanted to engage in debate. But when I never argued back but instead just loved her and showed interest in her life, I saw her soften.

It began when one day she liked a quote on my Facebook page by a Christian author. She made sure to inform me in the comment section that, even though the person who said the phrase believed in God, what they had to say still was inspiring to her. Pretty soon, she was not only liking inspiring quotes and thoughtful phrases, she actually clicked the "like" button on a few Bible verses! I had to chuckle to myself each time I saw one.

Then one day, we went out for lunch. I always tried to be respectful of her beliefs when we ate together, so I would bow my head quietly to say grace without speaking out loud so as not to offend her. But this time was different. When I bowed my head to say a silent prayer, she interrupted and told me it would be fine with her if I prayed aloud this time. And so I did. I not only thanked God for the delicious grilled chicken salads we were about to enjoy, I also thanked him for our friendship and for his allowing our paths to cross. I mentioned her fun personality and fierce love of her kids and husband. I told God I was grateful for her encouraging personality that is such a blessing in my life. When I looked up after uttering "Amen," I could see that she was visibly moved. Although she jokes about prayer, calling it "talking to the ceiling," I knew her heart was touched. And I continue to see her become more and more open to the gospel as our friendship grows.

Kindness rather than judgment. Choose it every time.

How to Sprinkle Love

Here are some discoveries I have made along the way when it comes to scattering kindness and pointing others to God.

SECURE YOUR INNER CIRCLE.

If you long to be a person who scatters God's kindness, surround yourself with others who have the same desire. You can share ideas, pray for each other, and encourage each other during those times when you think the effort simply isn't worth it. Christian support is crucial if you wish to live a life that follows and reflects Jesus.

ASK GOD TO HELP YOU DISCERN.

Reaching out to others can seem like an overwhelming task. Where do you begin? To whom should you seek to show kindness? Ask the Lord to help you start small, with just one simple gesture shown to one human soul. Living a life that is other-centered will be a constant journey of prayer. As you petition God for direction, you will not only be reaching out to others, you will be strengthening your relationship with him.

SEEK OUT DIVERSE RELATIONSHIPS.

How easy it is to only interact with those who look and live like us. Break through barriers to reach out to others who are different from you. Those who look different. Those who believe differently. Those whose varied interests and lifestyles are foreign to you. It may be scary at first, but it will enrich your life, and it will be a picture of the heaven that is to come. Eternity will be full of diverse people, and so our interactions here on earth should be as well.

START SMALL.

Kindness starts simply. An encouraging word. A loving gesture. A tender sentiment sent through the mail. A thoughtful small token. The gift of unhurried time. A rousing pep talk. Simply vowing to speak and act in a way that is gentle and kind is the starting point. Aesop was right: "No act of kindness, no matter how small, is ever wasted."

BE READY TO ANSWER ANYONE.

I used to get all worked up about talking to others about the gospel. My stomach knotted up. I experienced immense guilt because I was sure I wouldn't do it "right." I thought that every time I conversed with someone, I had to lay out a five-step process—complete with memorized Bible verses—on how to get to heaven. And then one day I happened upon a verse—1 Peter 3:15—that helped me to relax.

> But in your hearts revere Christ as Lord. Always be prepared to give an answer to everyone who asks you to give the reason for the hope that you have. But do this with gentleness and respect.

Maybe I didn't have to spend my time stressing and trying to "name drop" Jesus into a conversation. Maybe instead I needed to start praying that people would ask me the reason I seemed to have hope. And so I did. Oh boy, did that work! I can't tell you the number of times I have been able to share the gospel because someone asked me about how I live my life and how I seem to live it with hope. This doesn't mean we don't look for open doors of opportunity to work God into our conversations and share the gospel with people. It does mean we can stop putting so much pressure on ourselves, thinking it all depends on us. It doesn't. Which leads me to my final tip . . .

REMEMBER TO FOCUS ON OBEDIENCE.
LET GOD HANDLE THE OUTCOME.

Remember that your job is to be kind and willing to share the gospel with others. What happens as a result of your words and actions is up to God.

———— Listen. Love. Repeat. ————

It was just a simple bottle of perfume. I had purchased it half off on a clearance end cap at a local department store. It was one of my friend's favorite brands, and so I thought I would stash it away for her birthday coming up later that year. The next time I was at her house, however, I noticed she had more than a half-dozen bottles of perfume on her dresser, including nearly a full decanter of the kind I had purchased. And so the bottle sat waiting in my general store to be given to someone else, some other time.

My son had recently been getting to know a girl he was considering dating seriously. She had been over to our home a few times, and we were enjoying getting to know her too. As the story of her life unfolded, we discovered it was one that included much sorrow. A father who left the family over a decade ago, and with whom she had very little contact today. A mother who had been found dead in her bed one morning when this sweet gal was just a young teen. She had moved in with some family members to finish her schooling and to try her best to navigate the tumultuous teen years. After high school, she'd moved in with a friend's family as she attempted to figure out her future.

Valentine's Day was approaching, and my son wanted advice for what he might get this young lady. They weren't yet a serious couple, so he didn't want to choose a piece of jewelry or something else that might seem like he wanted a commitment. And so I advised him that maybe some flowers and a card and a bottle of perfume might be good. Since my son has more experience picking out a new baseball bat or cordless drill than selecting women's cosmetics, he asked me what brand of fragrance might be good to get. I mentioned the bottle I had purchased months earlier. And so he went "shopping" in my general store and reimbursed me for the price I had paid for the perfume.

There aren't many Valentine-worthy restaurants in our small town, so the two of them went out to a nice dinner in the nearby big city. After dinner, he presented her with the flowers and the card, along with some high-end chocolates for good measure. (Smart guy!) Then she reached into the bright fuchsia gift bag and lifted out the bottle of perfume.

Our son was not quite sure at first what the look on her face meant. She looked a little shocked and then began to cry. "How did you know?" she mumbled through her tears.

"Know what?" he asked, thoroughly puzzled.

"This is the perfume my mom always wore!" she said. She told him that she had not smelled it since her mom had passed away nearly a decade ago.

Only God would take a marked-down bottle of perfume and use it to touch a heart in such a special way.

Since that day, we have gotten to know this strong young woman even more. She spends time in our house. We pop popcorn with her and watch movies. We started taking her to church with us. Her first visit was the first time she had ever attended a service in her life. In fact, before she started hanging out with our family, she had no idea who Adam and Eve were. She had never heard of Noah and the ark. And although she knew all about the Easter bunny and colored eggs, she had never heard of the reality of Jesus dying on the cross for our sins.

We helped her to find a job, and we arranged for her to get some vocational advice from a couple we know who helps young adults plan strategically for their careers. We also helped locate a reliable but inexpensive used car so she can get to her job. We now know her favorite foods. And that she loves anything with chocolate and peanut butter. We are delighted by her contagious giggle as she sits around and enjoys a meal with us. She has become one of the family. And not just our family. God's family. Yes, a few weeks ago when she met with the couple we are friends with for a career counseling session, she gave her life to Christ in their living room, and became born again.

We have been honored to have a front row seat watching God change a life. And we have been privileged to play a small part in this story as we listened, loved, and then did it all over again.

There is nothing more thrilling than seeing a life changed for good and a heart turned toward God. As we scatter kindness, we help to create a safe space where we can openly share the gospel with others. We get to see a life change right before our eyes. Not only the life of another. But our lives as well.

Will you seek to live a life that scatters kindness? One that is other-centered rather than self-centered? One that listens and loves? If so, I pray that the boomerang of the blessing will come right back at you, showering you with a healthy dose of love and leaving you with a feeling of fulfillment.

I pray that in laying down your life for others, you find an even more satisfying one in return.

May I have the honor of praying for you?

Father, I thank you for the souls reading these words. May you empower them to live a life that not only places others above themselves but that points people to you as the way of salvation. In a world of darkness, may they be a flickering flame, shining light for you. In a culture of criticism and combativeness, may their words be encouraging and kind. Will you provide for them opportunities to share your love in seemingly simple ways? Most of all, grant them the privilege of seeing their simple gestures be used to bring about profound change. We love you. We want to be used by you. Help us to never be too busy to stop and notice. To listen. To love. And to repeat. In Jesus' name. Amen.

PRACTICE MAKES PERFECT

We've talked a lot about listening and loving. Now let's chat a bit about repeating. Hebrews 13:1 urges, "Keep on loving one another as brothers and sisters." The phrase *keep on* here in the original Greek is from the root word *meneto*, which means "to wait, stay, abide or remain." It is a verb—an action word. In a sense, it means to never stop showing up.

Often it's not the "one-off" things that make a difference. It's the consistency, the commitment, the showing up over and over and over again. Here are ways to "repeat" displaying love consistently:

♥ **Pick a person.** Is there someone, such as a librarian, package delivery person, or waiter who you see week in and week out? Be consistent. Each week when you see them, greet them heartily. Ask about how they are doing. Be interested in their life. If they perform a service, see if they need help. Or offer them refreshment. Our FedEx driver knows he can always count on me for a bottle of cold water or a soda on a hot summer day or some coffee in a to-go cup in the cold of winter. As you converse with them, take mental notes. Did they mention their son was trying out for the hockey team or their family was moving to a new house? Circle back around a few days or weeks later to inquire how the tryout went or to ask how they are coming with the unpacking and settling in at their new home. Listening and loving often lead to question asking.

♥ **Choose a cause.** Commit yourself to an issue or cause that touches your heart in some way, and make it a point to work on that cause weekly or monthly. My husband was the volunteer janitor for several years at a local pregnancy center. This saved the organization money because they didn't need to hire a cleaner. And our family regularly shows up to serve a hot meal at a halfway house for battered women and their kids. Then we provide childcare for the children while the moms take part in an evening

Bible study. What cause might you bless with your consistent care and attention?

♥ **Grab a group.** Are you part of a group that meets regularly? Come to the meetings as often as you can. Be on the alert for ways to show love in a group setting. Or be a constant source of help—arrive early to set up chairs or stay afterward to help put them away and clean up the room. Could you volunteer to be the one who solicits snacks each week so this task is taken off of the leader's plate? Mom's groups, Bible study groups, book study clubs, Sunday school classes, church small groups, school PTA organizations, neighborhood play groups, and many other such gatherings give you the chance to repeatedly show your love and concern, often just by showing up, listening, and offering to help make the group run!

♥ **Take the time.** Use time cues to remind you of the "repeat rule." Perhaps you kiss your husband every time he comes home from work. Or you have your family Bible reading time or a few moments of sharing about your day at the same time each evening. You might have a regularly scheduled coffee time with friends once a month when you listen to each other and exchange prayer requests. I start my teenage son's vehicle each morning, and before I send him off I ask him how I can be praying for his school day. Repetition builds commitment, gives you opportunities to listen . . . and demonstrates love!

Bonus Material

I hope this section will be an encouragement to you and equip you in your quest to listen, love, and then do it all over again! I have included relevant Bible verses on loving, some inspirational/motivational statements from the book, and also a few simple but delicious recipes—along with some cute tags to include with your food gift. May God bless you as you seek to scatter kindness in your corner of the world!

Memory Verses

FOR MAKING A DIFFERENCE

Here are some key verses of Scripture for you to commit to memory as you seek to be someone who listens, loves, and then does it all over again. You may wish to photocopy them on card stock and then cut them out. That way you can place them where you will see them often—on your car's dashboard, at your desk at work, at the kitchen sink, or on your bathroom mirror. (If they will be placed near water, you might want to laminate them as well.)

A new command I give you: Love one another. As I have loved you, so you must love one another. By this everyone will know that you are my disciples, if you love one another. *(John 13:34-35)*

My command is this: Love each other as I have loved you. Greater love has no one than this: to lay down one's life for one's friends. *(John 15:12-13)*

Be devoted to one another in love. Honor one another above yourselves. *(Romans 12:10)*

Let no debt remain outstanding, except the continuing debt to love one another, for whoever loves others has fulfilled the law. *(Romans 13:8)*

If anyone has material possessions and sees a brother or sister in need but has no pity on them, how can the love of God be in that person? Dear children, let us not love with words or speech but with actions and in truth.

(1 John 3:17-18)

Quips and Quotables

Here are some portions of the book that you may also wish to photocopy and keep nearby. They may serve as motivation for you to keep on sharing love with others.

Hearing a heart drop is an art we must lovingly cultivate. It can lead to the most wonderful times of encouragement as we make it our habit to listen and to love.

Jesus wasn't about doing big things. He was about doing the right thing. And often for him, the right thing was noticing *one simple soul.*

Jesus' real ministry *was the person he found standing in front of him. Who is that for you today? Rather than trying to do something grand for God, perhaps we need to embrace the obscure instead. To stop trying to be profound or important and instead* just be obedient.

WE DON'T DO GOOD FOR THE SAKE OF LOOKING GOOD; WE DO GOOD IN ORDER TO POINT OTHERS TO *Jesus.*

How might the Holy Spirit be tapping on your heart today, prompting you to speak truth, do good, and *share life?*

Don't do good works in order to selfishly shout, "Look at me!" Do them in order to humbly implore, "Will you look at him?"

Don't hang up on your relationships: hang in there instead.

LOVING OTHERS includes not just giving of our time but feeling with our hearts as well. Relationships require work. Remembering isn't always easy. And sometimes sweat is involved in LISTENING AND LOVING.

If our perspective each day can be "I am in it for you" *instead of* "What is in it for me?" *we will discover the joy of serving Jesus— without expecting anything in return and done only for an audience of One.*

We need to remember our *why:* the reason we love and serve and give thoughtful gifts and do good works. It is so that others will see Jesus. They may *look* at us, but we hope they *see* him.

Living a life of welcome—opening both
your heart and your home—means your stuff
gets used. And reused. Over and over again.
Your items get nicked and scratched. Your carpet
and rugs and linens get stained. While this doesn't
mean we don't try to make our surroundings
pleasant, it does mean we learn to accept some
degree of imperfection. Well-used items often
mean that we have loved well.

When we have a God-honoring perspective about our
possessions and resources, our hearts and homes
can become a *wheelhouse for ministry*. We can lead
with our hearts and bless with our homes, making our
homes a haven not only for those who dwell there
permanently but for whoever God sends our way.

WHEN WE WILLINGLY OPEN OUR HOMES,
WE AREN'T JUST BEING NICE. WE ARE
BEING OBEDIENT TO GOD'S WORD.

*If there is room in your heart, you'll
make room in your home.*

Whether you share a book or a bicycle, a cot
or a cottage, do it with an attitude of
OPENHANDEDNESS and OPENHEARTEDNESS,
sharing with others what God has given to you.

When we share love with
the lonely, the *boomerang of blessing*
lands right back in our lap.

♥

We might feel our life is boring
and our possessions are plain. Yet there are
many who would love to share our seemingly
mundane lives, simply to feel that they fit in
and that their presence is wanted.

♥

*SLOW AND STEADY wins the race to touch the
heart of the cantankerous. If you aren't praying
for the members of your family, who is?*

♥

SOMEHOW, FORGE A FAMILY.
Take all the irregular people that bear
your name and share your heritage.
God will place them together
in the most beautiful of ways,
FORMING A MONTAGE OF MAGNIFICENCE.
As we display love within the uniqueness
of our family, we show to the world
just how God draws us near,
WELCOMING WHO WE ARE.

♥

*Judgment does not win others over.
Kindness does.*

Kindness starts simply.

An encouraging word.

A loving gesture.

A tender sentiment sent through the mail.

A thoughtful small token.

The gift of unhurried time.

A rousing pep talk.

Simply vowing to speak and act in a way

that is gentle and kind is the starting point.

Aesop was right:

"No act of kindness, no matter how small, is ever wasted."

♥

Remember that your job is to be kind and willing to share the gospel with others. What happens as a result from your words and actions is up to God. Our job is obedience. *God's job is results.*

♥

As we scatter kindness, we help to create a safe space where we can openly share the gospel with others. We get to see a life change right before our eyes. Not only the life of another. But our lives as well.

Recipes

FOR REACHING OUT

Need an easy but delicious treat to give to someone to show them you care? Here are a few of our family's no-fail recipes along with some whimsical tags (provided right after the recipes) for you to photocopy, cut out, and include with your food gift. Simply use a hole-punch to make a hole in one corner of the tag and then thread some jute twine or thin ribbon through it and attach it to your goody. Enjoy!

Simple Cinnamon Rolls

A wonderful pick-me-up that will leave their taste buds delighted.

INGREDIENTS:

2 1/2 t. yeast (one package)
1/4 c. warm water (110–115 degrees)
1 c. whole milk
1/2 c. butter-flavored shortening
1/3 c. sugar
1 t. salt
1 large egg, beaten
4 c. (or more) bread flour
1/3 c. brown sugar
2 t. ground cinnamon
5 T. melted butter

ICING:

2 c. powdered sugar
2 T. butter, room temperature
¾ t. vanilla or orange extract
milk or cream, as needed

In a small bowl, dissolve yeast in warm water. In a large saucepan, heat milk over high heat until it just begins to boil. Remove from heat. Add shortening, sugar, and salt. Let cool until still slightly warm. Add yeast mixture and egg, and mix well. Add four cups or more bread flour, mixing well, until you have a soft but firm dough. Turn out onto a well-floured counter. Knead for 5 minutes. Place in a well-oiled bowl, cover with a towel, and let rise until doubled, about 1 ½ hours.

Turn onto a lightly floured surface. Roll into a rectangle about 10 x 14 inches. Brush with melted butter. Sprinkle on mixed brown sugar and cinnamon. Roll up, beginning with the short side, and place seam down on the counter. Cut into nine rolls. Place them in a greased 8-inch round pan with one in the center and the other eight spaced evenly around. Cover loosely with plastic wrap that has been sprayed with cooking spray to keep from sticking. Let rise 45 minutes to 1 hour.

Bake at 350 degrees for 18–23 minutes, or slightly longer, being careful to watch so they don't get too browned. Do NOT overbake. Cool. Blend icing ingredients together until smooth and spread over rolls. When frosting is set, wrap rolls in foil. Yum! ♥

Peanut-Butter Oatmeal Monster Cookies

I made a quadruple batch of these to send with my son's football team when they boarded the bus to football camp last summer. They were gone before the bus pulled out of the school parking lot!

INGREDIENTS:

½ c. salted butter, room temperature
    (do not use unsalted butter or margarine!)
¼ c. sugar
½ c. light brown sugar, packed
¾ c. creamy peanut butter
1 t. pure vanilla extract (not imitation)
2 medium eggs (or 1 large)
1 ¼ c. unbleached all-purpose flour
½ t. baking soda
½ c. quick-cooking oats (not old-fashioned oats)
½ c. regular M&M's
½ c. peanut butter M&M's
½ c. semi-sweet chocolate chunks

Preheat the oven to 350 degrees. Use parchment paper to line cookie sheets. (You may also bake them on an ungreased cookie sheet, but they turn out better on the parchment paper and as a bonus you will have no cleanup of the pans.)

In a stand mixer, or very large bowl using a handheld mixer, cream the butter and both sugars together until well blended. Add in the peanut butter and blend completely. Then mix in the vanilla and add eggs one at a time.

Measure the flour into the cups. For best results, do not scoop out the flour with the measuring cup as it packs too much flour in the cup. Instead, lightly spoon the flour into the measuring cups and then level off with a butter knife. Sprinkle the baking soda over the top of the flour and mix in just until combined. Be very careful not to overmix or the cookies will be tough.

Fold in the quick oats by hand, with a large wooden spoon or spatula.

Next, fold in the M&M's and the chocolate chunks. Cover the bowl with plastic wrap and chill for 30 minutes while you make yourself a cup of coffee or tea.

Using a tablespoon, scoop out dough and make balls about the size of a ping-pong ball. Place onto the parchment paper-lined baking sheets and press down slightly. Place a few extra M&M's on top if you like.

Bake 10–12 minutes, watching very closely. It is super important not to overbake them. They will actually appear to be underdone with the center looking a bit soft.

Remove the pans from the oven and let them cool 10–15 minutes before placing cookies on a wire cooling rack. They will be very soft and hard to work with, so be careful. They will firm up while they are cooling down.

You may store these cookies at room temperature in a covered container for up to five days. (That is, if they last that long!) They also freeze very well. You can also get them to the ball stage while they are still unbaked and flash-freeze them on cookie sheets by placing the balls on the sheets and freezing them for 2–3 hours. Then remove them from the freezer and place in gallon-sized freezer bags with a zip closure. Don't skip flash freezing. If you just put the balls straight into freezer bags without flash freezing, they will clump together. When you want to bake some fresh cookies from the frozen balls, you may remove them from the freezer and bake as instructed, adding a minute or two to the baking time. ♥

Chocolate Cherry Drop Cookies ∽

Reminds me of a chocolate-covered cherry. Chewy and delicious! A plate of these will disappear lickety-split.

IN A LARGE BOWL, CREAM:

1 stick butter
1 c. sugar
1 1/2 t. vanilla
1 egg

IN A MEDIUM BOWL, MIX:

1 1/2 c. flour
1/2 c. cocoa powder
1/4 t. salt
1/4 t. baking soda
1/4 t. baking powder

Drain one large jar maraschino cherries, setting aside juice.

Slowly add the dry ingredients to the wet ones just until incorporated and being careful not to overmix. Batter will be sticky, not stiff. Drop dough into heaping tablespoons on an ungreased cookie sheet. Push a cherry down into each.

BEFORE BAKING: frost each cookie with a teaspoon of the following frosting.

OVER VERY LOW HEAT, MELT:

6 oz. semi-sweet chocolate chips

ADD:

1/2 c. sweetened condensed milk
4 t. reserved cherry juice

Bake at 350 degrees for 10–12 minutes. Do not overbake. ♥

Pumpkin Bread ⌒〜

This is the most heavenly bread—with the perfect blend of sweetness and spices. I found it in an old 1960s cookbook I bought at an estate sale for a quarter. You're welcome.

IN A LARGE BOWL, BLEND:

3 1/2 c. pumpkin
3 1/2 c. sugar
1 c. oil
2 eggs

IN A MEDIUM BOWL, STIR TOGETHER:

4 c. all-purpose flour
1 1/2 t. cinnamon
1 1/2 t. salt
1 t. ground cloves
1/2 t. nutmeg
4 t. baking soda

Slowly add the dry ingredients to the wet ones just until incorporated and being careful not to overmix. Bake at 350 degrees for 1 hour in two large, greased loaf pans. Cool 15 minutes. Flip out of pans and cool for 20–30 minutes.

FROSTING:

2 c. powdered sugar
1/2 t. vanilla
half-and-half or whole milk

Combine powdered sugar and vanilla. Thin with half-and-half or whole milk until it is slightly thick but pourable. Drizzle frosting over top of the bread. When frosting is set, wrap in foil. ♥

Gift Tags

Photocopy any of these Scripture tags or sayings on card stock and cut them out. Use a hole-punch to make a hole and then thread jute twine or thin ribbon through and attach the tag to your food gift.

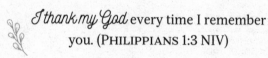

I thank my God every time I remember you. (PHILIPPIANS 1:3 NIV)

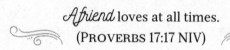

A friend loves at all times. (PROVERBS 17:17 NIV)

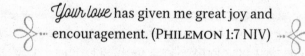

Your love has given me great joy and encouragement. (PHILEMON 1:7 NIV)

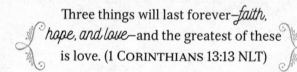

Three things will last forever—*faith, hope, and love*—and the greatest of these is love. (1 CORINTHIANS 13:13 NLT)

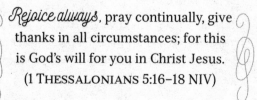

Rejoice always, pray continually, give thanks in all circumstances; for this is God's will for you in Christ Jesus. (1 THESSALONIANS 5:16–18 NIV)

Because you are a *blessing.*

Just because you are LOVED.

 You are in my prayers today.

I treasure our FRIENDSHIP.

 When I count my blessings,
I count you TWICE.

Can't IMAGINE life without you!

 I'm glad we are *family.*

I love you. THE END.

 YOU mean the world to me.

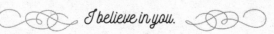 *I believe in you.*

 I thank GOD for you.

Notes

1. Laura Ingalls Wilder, *Little House in the Big Woods* (New York: Harper and Row, 1932).

2. Kay Warren, "Stop Sending Cheery Christmas Cards," *Christianity Today* (December 10, 2014), www.christianitytoday.com/ct/2014/december-web-only/kay-warren-stop-sending-cheery-christmas-cards.html?start=1

3. http://sacred-texts.com/bib/cmt/barnes/psa068.htm

4. http://wesley.nnu.edu/john-wesley/the-sermons-of-john-wesley-1872-edition/sermon-126-on-the-danger-of-increasing-riches/

About Karen

Karen Ehman is a *New York Times* bestselling author and a speaker for Proverbs 31 Ministries, as well as a writer for *Encouragement for Today*, online devotions that reach over one million women daily. She has authored ten books, including *Keep It Shut: What to Say, How to Say It, and When to Say Nothing at All* and *Let. It. Go.: How to Stop Running the Show and Start Walking in Faith* and is the coauthor with Ruth Schwenk of *Hoodwinked: Ten Myths Moms Believe and Why We All Need to Knock It Off* and *Pressing Pause: 100 Quiet Moments for Moms to Meet with Jesus.* Karen has been a guest on a number of television and radio programs, including *The 700 Club, At Home Live, FamilyLife, Engaging Women, The Harvest Show, Moody Midday Connection*, and *Focus on the Family*.

Karen has been married for over a quarter century to her college sweetheart, Todd, and together they have raised their three sometimes quarrelsome but mostly charming children in the boondocks of central Michigan. There she enjoys antique hunting, cheering for the Detroit Tigers baseball team, and processing life with family, friends, and the many teens and young adults that gather around her kitchen island for a taste of Mama Karen's cooking.

You can connect with her at karenehman.com, where she helps women to live their priorities and love their lives. For booking information on Karen's speaking, call 877-731-4663 or visit proverbs31.org/speakers.

Proverbs 31
MINISTRIES

About Proverbs 31 Ministries

If you were inspired by *Listen, Love, Repeat* and desire to deepen your relationship with God—or if you would like to have Karen speak at your event—we encourage you to connect with Proverbs 31 Ministries.

Proverbs 31 Ministries exists to be a trusted friend who will take you by the hand and walk by your side, leading you one step closer to the heart of God through:

- Free online daily devotions delivered automatically to your email inbox
- First 5, a free mobile device app that delivers a five minute daily Bible study first thing in the morning
- Online Bible studies
- A daily radio program
- COMPEL writers training community (compeltraining.com)
- Books and resources
- The She Speaks Conference for writers, speakers, and women in ministry

To learn more about Proverbs 31 Ministries, visit www.proverbs31.org. For booking information for Karen's speaking, call 877-731-4663 or visit proverbs31.org/speakers.

Proverbs 31 Ministries
630 Team Road, Suite 100
Matthews, NC 28105
www.proverbs31.org

Listen, Love, Repeat
Study Guide with DVD

Other-Centered Living in a Self-Centered World

Karen Ehman

Because the normal default is to look out for number one, to become a person who thinks about others first will take great effort on our part. It requires us to live alert. To be on the lookout for what Karen calls "heart drops," stealthily stowed comments in conversations with others that give us a hint into what kindness we might grant them. And also to notice those in our lives who might need a helping hand, a generous dose of encouragement, or a loving gesture done with no expectation of a return favor.

In this six-session video study, engaging Bible teacher Karen Ehman looks at scriptural examples of those who lived alert (among them Abraham, Abigail, the Good Samaritan, and of course Jesus himself, who noticed those who least expected to be noticed). Through these examples, women will be inspired to live alert and to realize that in order to find joy in life, we must learn to stop focusing on ourselves and seek to make someone else's life better instead.

Additionally, this inspiring and practical study provides encouragement and ideas for reaching out to others with both planned and random acts of kindness. Topics include loving your family and friends, encouraging coworkers, reaching out to the lonely, and blessing the "necessary people," those individuals who help you get life done every day but often go unnoticed.

The study guide includes video notes, group discussion questions, memory verses, weekly challenges, between-sessions personal studies, and ideas for a bonus session seven wrap-up party.

Available in stores and online!

Hoodwinked

Ten Myths Moms Believe & Why We Need To Knock It Off

Karen Ehman and Ruth Schwenk

Moms have been hoodwinked—tricked into believing lies that keep them from not only enjoying motherhood but forging friendships with other moms who might tackle the tasks of motherhood differently. Myths such as "Mothering is natural, easy, and instinctive" cause moms to feel like failures if they have questions or apprehensions in raising their kids. Operating from the premise that "The way I mother is the right (and only) way" puts up fences between moms instead of building bridges of encouragement between them. Lies such as "I am my child's choices" tempt moms to mistakenly believe that if their child makes a wrong choice then they, in turn, must be a bad mom.

In their encouraging "we've been there" style, Karen Ehman and Ruth Schwenk enable mothers to:

- Identify ten myths of motherhood
- Replace the lies with the truth of what God says
- Acquire practical tools to help them form new and improved thought patterns and healthy behaviors
- Forge healthy, supportive relationships with other moms of all ages and stages
- Confidently embrace the calling of motherhood as they care for their families in their own unique way

Six-session DVD study also available.

Keep It Shut

What to Say, How to Say It, and When to Say Nothing at All

Karen Ehman

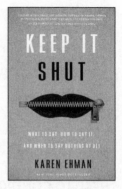

From Bible times to modern times, women have struggled with their words. What to say and how to say it. What not to say. When it is best to remain silent. And what to do when you've said something you wish you could now take back. In this book a woman whose mouth has gotten her into loads of trouble shares the hows (and how-not-tos) of dealing with the tongue.

Beyond just a "how not to gossip" book, this book explores what the Bible says about the many ways we are to use our words and the times when we are to remain silent. Karen will cover using our speech to interact with friends, coworkers, family, and strangers as well as in the many places we use our words in private, in public, online, and in prayer. Even the words we say silently to ourselves. She will address unsolicited opinion-slinging, speaking the truth in love, not saying words just to people-please, and dealing with our verbal anger.

Christian women struggle with their mouths. Even though we know that Scripture has much to say about how we are—and are not—to use our words, this is still an immense issue, causing heartache and strain not only in family relationships, but also in friendships, work, and church settings.

Available in stores and online!

Let. It. Go.

How to Stop Running the Show and Start Walking in Faith

Karen Ehman

Doable ideas, thought patterns, and tools to help you LET GO OF YOUR NEED TO CONTROL

The housework. The meals. The kids. Many women are wired to control. But trying to control everything can be exhausting, and it can also cause friction with your friends and family.

This humorous yet thought-provoking book guides you as you discover the freedom and reward of living a life "out of control," in which you allow God to be seated in the rightful place in your life. Armed with relevant biblical and current examples (both to emulate and to avoid), doable ideas, new thought patterns, and practical tools to implement, *Let. It. Go.* will gently lead you out of the land of over control into a place of quiet trust.

A companion video-based study for small groups is also available.

Available in stores and online!